COME TO THE FEAST

Liturgical Theology
of, by, and *for* Everybody

Michael Kwatera, O.S.B.

LITURGICAL PRESS
Collegeville, Minnesota

www.litpress.org

Abundant thanks to Dr. Patrick Henry, former director of the Institute for Ecumenical and Cultural Research at Saint John's, Collegeville, Minnesota, for his careful editorial work on this manuscript.

Cover design by David Manahan, O.S.B. Cover photograph courtesy of Michael Jensen Photography.

Illustration on page 13 from Clemens Schmidt, *Clip Art for the Liturgical Year* (Collegeville: Liturgical Press, 1988) 101.

The English translation of the Preface for Weekdays IV from *The Roman Missal* © 1973, International Committee on English in the Liturgy, Inc. All rights reserved.

1   2   3   4   5   6   7   8

Library of Congress Cataloging-in-Publication Data

Kwatera, Michael.
    Come to the feast : liturgical theology of, by, and for everybody / Michael Kwatera.
        p.   cm.
    Summary: "Celebrates and affirms the valuable and necessary ministry of laywomen and laymen in the liturgy"—Provided by publisher.
    Includes bibliographical references and index.
    ISBN-13: 978-0-8146-1521-8 (pbk. : alk. paper)
    ISBN-10: 0-8146-1521-X (pbk. : alk. paper)
    1. Laity—Catholic Church.   2. Mass.   I. Title

BX1920.K88   2005
264'.02–dc22

2005013486

For Allan Bouley, O.S.B.,
my confrere at Saint John's Abbey,
with gratitude for helping me
to be a teacher and practitioner of Christian liturgy

Contents

Introduction: The People's Work Once Again 8

PART I: HOSPITALITY

    1. The Church Door Speaks 12

    2. Bed, Table, Chair, and Lamp:
       God Really Loves to Have Us 14

PART II: WHO'S HERE?

    3. Guests and Servants 24

    4. In Company with Angels and Archangels 33

PART III: WHAT HAPPENS?

    5. The Waiting Lord 38

    6. Changing Water into Wine 44

PART IV: WHO DO WE BECOME?

    7. The Ministry Quilt 48

    8. Chosen Race, Royal Priesthood, Holy People 52

PART V: WHAT HAPPENS NEXT?

    9. We Have Seen the Lord 58

    10. Prayers for the Journey 68

Introduction:

The People's Work Once Again

I admit I am discouraged by what I judge to be lack of progress in liturgical renewal since the Second Vatican Council—and I know I'm not the only one. But sometimes my drooping spirit is revived. My friend, Msgr. Kenneth Hedrick, wrote in his St. Anselm parish bulletin in Madisonville, Louisiana, about a workshop I led for the altar servers in 1988:

> Father Mike began the session by giving a brief explanation of how it takes teamwork to make good liturgy happen. We both wondered if this was making any sense at all to these young people. But, when we began actually walking through the order of the Mass with them, to show them how to serve, we knew that they were leagues ahead of us. Father Mike served as the presider and we assigned two of the youth to serve and asked the others to watch. They knew better. Watching is not what liturgy is about.
>
> Mary quickly picked up a book and got in line with the procession to be the reader. After a few shots at that, she moved on and became choir director. Several others joined her in the choir's chairs and la-la-la'd during the practice *Presentation of the Gifts*. Bret, Eric and Josh made attempts at tickling the ivories. Donovan replaced Mary as the reader and Timothy came forward to deacon. He even knew the parts! (He and Donovan are a bit ambitious: they soon became concelebrants!)
>
> Our young people well knew that liturgy is a group activity—and they readily jumped into action. It was worship at play and they play it well. In the reform of the liturgy, the bishops of the world at the Second Vatican Council called for reforms to promote "full, conscious and active participation" by all. Our young people have well gotten that message. They are being shaped into and responding as joyful participants in prayer. Michael and I were touched and amazed.

Yes, I was. These children showed me how formative the renewed liturgy has been. They know that liturgical ministry is an expected, ordinary, and familiar part of Roman Catholic worship. Msgr. Ken concluded: "Isn't it amazing how much our children have to teach us?"

It used to be—indeed, in the living memory of many still active today—that you went to church to see something happen, something done by someone else in a language you didn't comprehend. You may have understood that it was in some sense *about* you, but there was no reason to think it was something you *did*. Then came the Second Vatican Council.

Suddenly the Eucharist became an action of the whole assembly in the language you used every day. Spectators became actors, and the liturgy became something you did that was not only about you but also about everyone else in the room and everyone else in all the rooms on earth. You don't just *go to* church. You *are* church.

This book celebrates and affirms the valuable, necessary ministry of laypersons in the liturgy, for every liturgical ministry somehow deepens our sharing in God's saving grace. The focus will occasionally be on particular liturgical ministries—for example, lector or greeter—but these are only particular instances of every Christian's responsibility and privilege.

The most profound insistence of Vatican Council II—not something new, but recovery of a truth as old as the Bible itself—is this: We live a life of God's favor because of our baptism. That preeminent act of God's favor began with these words: "The Christian community welcomes you with great joy." We enjoy God's hospitality within the liturgy because there God gathers us to celebrate the favor we enjoy as heirs with Christ through baptism.

God's invitation to be at home within our church community and its house of worship, to enjoy God's lavish hospitality in Word and sacrament, does not depend on any previous merit, status, or accomplishment of ours. Our great dignity results from God's free gift of holiness in our dying and rising with Christ that begins in baptism and lasts a lifetime. The community where we live in the power of this dying and rising is born of God's hospitality to us in baptism; that community is continually reborn and renewed through God's hospitality to us in the Eucharist. The hospitality that God showed us at our baptism is renewed for us often in the words and gestures of those who serve the assembly of the baptized at the Eucharist, and in the hospitable actions and attitudes of everyone present.

God's best hospitality is a humble meal to be shared and served by humble people, by those who leave special claims of privilege and self-importance behind. At this banquet, VIPs and nobodies (in the world's eyes, not God's) hear the same Word and receive the same Lord, the Lord of all. A humble, grateful heart is the only requirement. "Everyone can come, just as you are," is the liturgy's invitation which sounds in the ears of sinners and saints alike. And aren't all of us really both? Thus the liturgical assembly is the self-expression of humanity as it is and as it is called to be. It is the privileged task of liturgical ministers to help the assembly become the Body of Christ, and then, having become anew the Body of Christ, all go forth to serve his members in the world more faithfully.

One of the strong vital signs of the assembly today is the prevalence of laypersons exercising ministerial roles within it. Twenty years ago, the *Notre Dame Study of Catholic Parish Life* reported that "lay communion ministers function at 70% of Sunday Masses and 64% of Saturday evening celebrations" examined in the study.[1] Such welcome developments have helped to make the liturgy the "people's work" once again. This is why Pope John Paul II reminded us that "it is more necessary than ever to promote the liturgical life within our communities, *through an adequate formation of the ministers and of all the faithful,* in view of that full, conscious and active participation in the liturgical celebrations envisioned by the Council."[2]

---

[1] Mark Searle and David C. Leege, *Notre Dame Study of Catholic Parish Life,* No. 5: The Celebration of Liturgy in the Parishes, August, 1985, 3.

[2] *Apostolic Letter of the Supreme Pontiff John Paul II on the 40th Anniversary of the Constitution "Sacrosanctum concilium" on the Sacred Liturgy,* no. 7 (italics added).

PART I

HOSPITALITY

1

The Church Door Speaks

"Greetings in Christ Jesus! I am the door to your parish church. My first name is 'Welcome.' I draw you into your holy house for worship by means of a certain mystery. I draw you into a sacred meeting with your God and with each other.

"Newborn babies pass through me on their way to the font of rebirth. Those born into everlasting life pass through me on the way to their place of rest. Beginnings and endings and resting places along life's journey: I am part of them all, because I am the door to the assembly for worship.

"That is why I rejoice to take my place in a distinguished family of doors:

- the door to the home at Bethany, where Lazarus, Martha, and Mary offered hospitality to the Lord Jesus;
- the door to the tax collector Zacchaeus' house, where that repentant sinner welcomed the Lord Jesus;
- the door to the house in Capernaum, where the sick came for healing from the Lord Jesus;
- the door to the upper room, where bread and wine became the sacred Body and Blood of the Lord Jesus;
- the door to the empty tomb, where angels announced the resurrection of the Lord Jesus.

"Yes, all those doors were hallowed by the Lord Jesus as he passed through them. But today, the members of his Body in this world, his holy sisters and brothers, pass through me, the door to their church, to meet Jesus there. And I welcome you, all of you, to this worshiping assembly. Yes, all of you, especially those who might be overlooked and ignored.

"I remember one Holy Thursday, at the evening Mass of the Lord's Supper. After the latecomers had hurried through me and taken their seats, I surveyed the carefully rehearsed and nearly flawlessly executed ceremonies. I admired the shimmering vestments and banners, reveled in the soaring clouds of fragrant incense and soft light of flickering candles, and even hummed along as the melodious praise rose heavenward from organ, choir, and congregation. Then I happened to observe a father and his mentally challenged son approach, quietly enter the church, and take seats in the front of the assembly. And I thought to myself: 'Now the banquet is complete.'

"No matter how glorious the furnishings, ceremonies, or music may be, it is the faith of the poorest and weakest members of Christ's Body—those closest to his heart—that confirms the liturgical assembly as a source of richness and strength for all.

"It's true that I, the church door, draw people into that assembly. But without you, God's people, I am only a door, beautiful to the eye, perhaps, but lacking something crucial: *you*, members of the Body of Christ, believers who are called to worship God within the assembly and to serve each other outside it. You give God's hospitality a human face and human words and human gestures in a way that no door ever can.

"Jesus said: 'I am the door. Whoever enters through me will be saved.' I, the door to your parish church, represent this in wood and metal and glass. But you, God's beloved children, do the same, in flesh and blood. You enter the church as individuals; there Christ forms you into a community gathered in his name. And there, through your participation in the words and songs and actions and sacred food of the Eucharist, you minister to each other. I, the door to your church, am part of this ministry, for mine is a silent invitation to become part of the assembly, to be right in the middle of all that it says and does. But you, the assembly, bring my ministry to fulfillment.

"Oh, did I tell you my last name? It's 'Come Again.'"

2

Bed, Table, Chair, and Lamp:
God Really Loves to Have Us

One day Elisha came to Shunem, where there was a woman of influence, who urged him to dine with her. Afterward, whenever he passed by, he used to stop there to dine. So she said to her husband, "I know that he is a holy man of God. Since he visits us often, let us arrange a little room on the roof and furnish it for him with a bed, table, chair, and lamp, so that when he comes to us he can stay there." Sometime later Elisha arrived and stayed in the room overnight.

Later Elisha asked, "Can something be done for her?"

"Yes!" Gehazi answered. "She has no son, and her husband is getting on in years." "Call her," said Elisha. When she had been called, and stood at the door, Elisha promised, "This time next year you will be fondling a baby son" (2 Kgs 4:8-11, 14-16).

Great was the dignity in her face and in her step as she and her husband climbed the outside stairway from the garden. Once inside the newly added and well-furnished room atop their house, she proudly surveyed the scene and exclaimed: "See, it's all ready! And it's really splendid, if I do say so myself! Just smell that sweet balm in the air! There's plenty of wine, oil, and honey . . . and such lovely dates in the big bowl there on the table. Do you think the holy man will like the bright bedspread? All this will be for his use as often and as long as he likes. When that weary traveler passes this way again, we'll ask him— beg him!—to spend the night here. He can't refuse, can he?"

No, Elisha didn't refuse. This cool, quiet, and private upper room, with its lovely view of the rich grain fields surrounding Shunem, became a favorite and frequent retreat for the prophet when he stopped there enroute to the neighboring towns. The Shunammite woman had established the world's first "bed and breakfast," and Elisha had it all to himself. No matter how exhausted he might be from ministering in one village after another, he was assured of a pleasant room of his own at the home of his generous hosts.

Why did the woman provide these comfortable lodgings? She couldn't expect to get any tax write-off for charitable work and contributions, but she probably hoped for something better. The woman knew that she would do well to observe the ancient Semitic etiquette of hospitality, especially toward a holy man like Elisha. He breathed forth a spirit of soothing, healing beneficence wherever he walked, and he was known all over Israel for powerfully doing God's work. So the thought came to her: "If I provide him a place for rest and meditation, might not some of his holiness rub off on me in the form of a blessing?" Yet perhaps she feared that such extraordinary holiness would make it unsafe to entertain the prophet in the family quarters, and so a room *apart* from the rest of the house would prevent potentially dangerous contact with him (the spiritual equivalent of trying to keep a safe distance from high-voltage power lines). Or perhaps it's more reasonable to assume that the room apart was simply the woman's way of offering permanent and comfortable hospitality to the prophet, but not without a tiny bit of selfishness on her part: she believed that his presence would bring a blessing to her home.

She was right, but the blessing that she was to receive was nothing like what she was expecting. Elisha learned that she and her husband had wanted a son, although they had given up hope of having one. He now assured her that a son would be hers, and the following spring the woman gave birth to the son whom Elisha had promised. This was the first of the blessings that Elisha brought to the woman's hospitable home. Her story shows that her words and deeds of hospitality, which reflect the Hebrew Bible's best thinking on this virtue, had a profound and lasting influence for good in her life and in the lives of others.

In the King James Version of the Bible, the Shunammite woman is called "great" (2 Kgs 4:8). This undoubtedly means that she was a woman of wealth and influence. But she was especially great in providing the best of hospitality for her guests. Hospitality has been defined as "kindness to strangers," and Elisha's host excelled in this life-giving art.

Hospitality is an outward expression of an inner love for others, whether that expression be lavish or simple, elegant or plain. The modest accommodations of bed, table, chair, and lamp that the woman provided for the prophet Elisha could never match those we expect to find today in even mediocre motels, but they certainly provided him with the basics of Middle-Eastern hospitality at that time. And even today, what traveler among us hasn't relished the welcome refreshment of a comfortable bed after a long, tiring day of travel? Who hasn't been grateful for the welcome presence of a table or desk in one's lodging, so that one can write postcards to family and friends or share a snack with a companion? Who hasn't delighted in the welcome comfort of a chair in which to read the newspaper or the Bible, or to snooze awhile? Who hasn't welcomed the light of a lamp, whose gentle brightness invites hours of pleasant conversation among friends, long into the night?

Such are the welcome pleasures of what may be called "physical" hospitality: the care that our hosts provide for our physical needs. And yet, such physical hospitality really is only the outward expression of their inner love and care for our entire well-being: what may be called "spiritual" hospitality, a kindness that is present in the hearts of those who love us and which becomes outwardly visible and tangible on various occasions, in various ways.

When it comes to "spiritual" hospitality, there is no one more hospitable than God. There is a basic yet lavish hospitality that God shows us Sunday by Sunday as we celebrate the Eucharist together in our church. God extends an invitation to each of us to gather with our sisters and brothers in a beautiful, well-furnished room that God has prepared for us. And as we recall the woman's hospitality for the prophet Elisha, does she not show us something of how our God acts toward us? For just as she hustled and bustled to prepare fit lodgings for the holy man of God, so our God eagerly prepares divine hospitality for God's holy ones—yes, for you and me!—each Sunday in a holy house.

Here God gives us all the basics of hospitality for our spiritual enjoyment. Not a bed, but a time and place for Sunday's welcome refreshment of soul and spirit after a tiring week, an oasis for our days in the desert, an opportunity to rest awhile in God's presence. Some worshipers in Puritan New England used to find the long sermons so restful that the assistants had to wake them by tapping their heads with rods.

"I have stilled my soul, hushed it like a weaned child" says the Psalmist (Ps 131:2). Maybe that's what the patriarch Jacob did before his truly divine sleep in the shrine at Bethel, during which he had a dream of angels and heard the voice of the Lord (Gen 28:10-22). But unlike Jacob, we don't have to roll out our sleeping bags and prop up a stone for a pillow in order to discover the restful place of God's abode and hear the reassuring words of God's love. Our church is the house of God where can discover God's presence in the gracious words and gestures of greeting as we enter for worship, in the beauty of the liturgical environment that draws us into the celebration, and in the various ministries of our fellow worshipers during the liturgy. Liturgical ministers help to reveal God's presence by the divine service that they share with the angelic ministers ascending and descending the stairway in Jacob's dream (Gen 28:12). The liturgy's sacred words and gestures join heaven to earth within the assembly, but not without each person's imperfect but necessary ministry.

Jacob's faith in God was renewed and deepened by his brief stay in a sacred place, and so is ours. Even if your church sits right next to a busy thoroughfare, God can make it an "out of the way place" where we find the refreshment that Jesus invites us to enjoy (see Mark 6:30)—for those who are tired, rest; for those who are heavy laden, burdens lifted by the power of God's Word and sacrament. Then we can say with Jacob: "Truly, the Lord is in this place!" (Gen 28:16).

God sets a table—the altar from which we receive and serve a sacred banquet, food of travelers, pledge of everlasting life. The General Instruction of the Roman Missal, with its prescriptions and rubrics for the celebration of the Eucharist, says that "the altar on which the Sacrifice of the Cross is made present under sacramental signs is also the table of the Lord to which the People of God is called together to participate in the Mass, as well as the center of the thanksgiving that is accomplished through the Eucharist" (no. 296). Because the altar is the center of the assembly's thankful praise, it becomes a primary focus of the assembly's prayerful attention right from the first moments of the liturgy. Balthasar Fischer explains that by kissing the altar, the priest really is saying that "there are many tables in the world around which families gather for meals, and they are all good, but there is one of them that must be praised above all other tables on earth: the Lord's table, the table at which the Lord ever anew prepares his mysterious sacrificial meal and offers it to us."[3]

---

[3] Balthasar Fischer, *Signs, Words & Gestures: Short Homilies on the Liturgy*, Matthew J. O'Connell, trans. (New York: Pueblo Publishing, 1981) 21.

Thus, "the altar is more than a piece of liturgical furniture needed for Mass . . . it is a place which every Christian must regard as holy and deserving of praise and love. It is not just any table, but the table of the Lord from which our real life is constantly fed."[4] Shouldn't we be especially reverent toward the sacred table, treating it with the same degree of reverence that we accord to the Body and Blood of Christ? And must not our reverence for the table which receives the Body and Blood of Christ be matched by our concern for the suffering members of that Body? John Chrysostom, the early fifth century patriarch of Constantinople, noted that his congregation generously gave money and precious gifts for the place of worship, but he asked:

> Is there any point in his [Christ's] table being laden with golden cups while he himself is perishing from hunger? First fill him when he is hungry and then set his table with lavish ornaments. Are you making a golden cup for him at the very moment when you refuse to give him a cup of cold water? Do you decorate his table with cloths flecked with gold, while at the same time you neglect to give him what is necessary for him to cover himself?[5]

To receive and minister the holy gifts of God at the altar commits us to spread a generous table before the poor.

God gives us a chair—well, probably a seat in a pew in most churches. The God who has already given us spiritual seats with Christ in the heavens (Eph 2:6) now gives us a place in the sacred assembly of God's people at worship. The African-American spiritual, "Deep River," asks us chillun if we don't "want to go, to that gospel feast, / That promised land, that land, where all is peace? / [I want to] Walk into heaven, and take my seat. . . ." Well, we do hope to have a seat at the heavenly banquet, but on the way there, we pause to sit a bit along the route.

The statement *Environment and Art in Catholic Worship* explains that "benches or chairs for seating the assembly should be so constructed and arranged that they maximize the feelings of community

---

[4] Ibid., 21–22.

[5] Chrysostom, *On Matthew: Homily 50.4,* quoted in William J. Walsh, S.J., and John P. Langan, S.J., "Patristic Social Consciousness—The Church and the Poor," in *The Faith That Does Justice: Examining the Christian Sources for Social Change,* John C. Haughey, S.J., ed. (New York/Ramsey/Toronto: Paulist Press, 1977) 131.

and involvement" (no. 68). This accords with the statement in the General Instruction of the Roman Missal that "The faithful and the choir should have a place that facilitates their active participation" (no 294). The priest celebrant and other ministers "have places in the sanctuary" (no. 294). This part of the church "is where the altar stands, where the Word of God is proclaimed, and where the priest, the deacon, and the other ministers exercise their offices" (General Instruction, no. 295).

This "hierarchical" emphasis is intended to differentiate and highlight complementary ministries within the liturgy. Yet it is especially fitting for lectors and extraordinary ministers of Holy Communion to sit within the assembly until their particular ministry requires their presence in the sanctuary. Thus they highlight their essential unity with the people they serve.

Such unity in the worship space manifests God's ultimate purpose in gathering the worshipers together: to give the world a vision of God's victory in Christ over all human divisions and inequalities. Every seat in the sacred assembly of God's people (even the popular back pews that some parishioners try to steal from the ushers) is a place of honor for the guests whom God has invited to the feast in honor of the beloved Son. There are no second-class citizens within our liturgy, no second-class seats.

Last but not least, God sets a lamp before us. The Psalmist declares, "Your word is a lamp for my feet, a light for my path" (Ps 119:105). The Word of God, proclaimed and preached on in the liturgy, truly is the unfailing light for our days and ways. Sunday after Sunday, the God who lighted the two great lamps of sun and moon lights the greater lamp of God's Word for our understanding and guidance.

The flame of the small pottery saucer-lamp in the prophet Elisha's room was tiny indeed, yet how powerfully it pushed back night's darkness. We moderns can turn night into day through our wonders of artificial lighting, yet how great our age's *spiritual* darkness can be! Thus we do well to pray that the gladdening light of God's Word will guide us safely to the heavenly dwelling place.

That light is brightest in Jesus Christ. In him, the light of God's truth "bestows sight to the darkness of sinful eyes" (Alternative Opening Prayer for Ash Wednesday). His death and resurrection have set him as the ever-burning lamp of God's holy city in heaven, the beacon for pilgrims in God's holy Church on earth.

Lamps in the time of Elisha were often kept burning all day so that one could kindle a fire at will, and they burned all night, too. The liturgical assembly is illumined by such an eternal lamp: the Word of God proclaimed in the Scriptures. The Christ who speaks to us in his Word is the light that darkness can never overcome (John 1:5), the one who turns darkness into the light of life for his followers (John 8:12). Such is the light that burns brightly in the hearts of those who proclaim and hear that Word, those human temples sanctified by the Spirit of God.

At the Last Supper, Jesus prayed to his Father: "Consecrate them in the truth. Your word is truth" (John 17:17). The ministry of those who proclaim and preach the Word of God, and the receptivity of those who hear it and take it in (Matt 13:23), are part of the process of consecration through that Word, and liberation, too. The ministry of the Word lifts a torch of liberty that is infinitely brighter than the one Miss Liberty lifts beside the "golden door." The Word of God, reverently held and lovingly spoken, brings freedom from the works of darkness and death. Proclamation of the Scriptures should help keep the assembly's attention fixed on the Word of God, as on a lamp shining in the darkest places of their lives (see 2 Pet 1:19).

As a child, I was taught that the two altar candles at "Low Mass" represented the Old and New Testaments. Since that idea might now seem hyper-symbolizing, I suggest another: the candles that burn in the sanctuary can symbolize the ministry of the Word that dispels the darkness of hearts and minds. And as the Spirit who speaks to us in the Scriptures makes our hearts "glow with pure light" (Solemn Blessing for Pentecost), we ourselves begin to shine as the light of the world, just as Jesus promised (Matt 5:14-16). Aidan Kavanagh correctly reminds us that whereas the reader

> serves the assembly by reading a lesson, he or she thereby serves the assembly even beyond the time of worship by having placed before it the example of one who is palpably and publicly concerned with God's Word. The reader is someone who not only reads texts in public but embodies the Word for the assembly's benefit. . . . Ministers make ministry concrete both in their function and in their own life. Quality of function and quality of life cannot be separated in the liturgical minister without disservice to the assembly.[6]

---

[6] Aidan Kavanagh, *Elements of Rite: A Handbook of Liturgical Style* (New York: Pueblo Publishing, 1982) 38, 39.

There must be a basic, vital bond between service of God and God's people within the liturgy and service of others outside it. Only in this way can lectors and preachers truly bear the lamp of God's Word that gives light to all in the house and fills them with the dawning brightness of God's reign. Through their ministry, the earthly assembly becomes "a symbolization or self-expression of the heavenly assembly, of those who are gathered in the kingdom to celebrate eternally God's creative Word and unitive Love."[7]

A place of rest, a table, a seat, a lamp. Now that we have surveyed the liturgical accommodations that God has provided for us, we might ask about our qualifications to have them. When were we invited? Are we really entitled to enjoy them? Yes, but only because of our baptism.

Sunday after Sunday, God renews the gift of life made to us at our baptism by human expressions of divine hospitality: within our churches, at our altars, in our seats, in God's Word. The marks of divine hospitality, given through human words and gestures, are for all the followers of Jesus, even superficial or weak ones. Jesus wouldn't want it any other way. Jesus' life gave to the Church at its beginning the hospitality of God, a love that welcomes each person into the reign of God. It is from his life that the assembly understands the meaning of reconciliation, of healing, of eating and sharing with the poor and sinners. Jesus' Gospel testifies that "the kingdom is present with its peace and salvation where Pharisee and prostitute, righteous and unrighteous, easterner and westerner, northerner and southerner, prodigal and responsible, rich and poor, tax collector and prophet sit at table and break bread with one another."[8] Jesus' lordship "is attained through a cross and expressed in a meal—an act of hospitality, peace, brotherhood and sisterhood. His kingship is known in the time of the Church, as in the time of earthly life, in acts of service and in the reception of the sinner, the straying, the poor, the outcast, the despised, the wanderer and the stranger."[9] Thus the assembly's worship is rehearsal for God's final day, the day of the Lord:

---

[7] James Dallen, *Gathering for Eucharist: A Theology of Sunday Assembly* (Old Hickory, Tenn.: Pastoral Arts Associates of North America, 1982) 60.

[8] Robert Smith, *Easter Gospels* (Minneapolis: Augsburg Publishing, 1983) 121.

[9] Ibid., 122.

> While the assembly contains sinners and itself sins against its members and betrays its call and inner life, the processes of its activity symbolize redeemed humanity gathering into one, listening attentively and obediently to the voice of God, sharing in love and mutual concern the gifts of creation and salvation, and seeking to sum up in itself the goal of all creation.[10]

Such is God's kindness toward us in the liturgy, glimpsed through the elements of a great lady's hospitality toward the prophet Elisha. The offering of God's gifts of hospitality to others is not a duty to be performed, but rather a way of life to be lived, both within the assembly and outside it. And like Elisha's gracious host, we receive something in return for what we give.

The blessing that the woman gave Elisha by caring for his needs came back to her unexpectedly in the birth of her son. The woman gave the prophet some of the earthly riches that God had given her; God responded with the heavenly gift of a child. Don't we also receive unexpected, heavenly blessings as we extend God's hospitality in the assembly? All our words and deeds of hospitality—dressing the house for worship, welcoming our sisters and brothers, proclaiming the Scriptures, performing the music as prayer, ministering the Body and Blood of Christ, and simply being an active participant in the assembly's worship—do these not bring us the blessings of deeper faith in God and greater love for God? And who has not felt their love for God's people renewed and deepened in the very doing of acts of hospitality?

As we extend God's gracious hospitality to our fellow travelers in the liturgy, a miracle happens. There is born within us a new appreciation for God's loving-kindness given to the assembly and then, through the assembly, to the whole world. Mark Searle highlights the service to the world that is the assembly's task until the return of its Lord: "The assembly, remembering Christ in a profound act of recollection, discovers its own mystery, its identity as the Body of Christ in the world, continuing his surrender to God and to the work of God, until the end of time ('ready to greet him when he comes again')."[11]

---

[10] Dallen, 55–56.

[11] Mark Searle, "Assembly: Remembering the People of God," *Pastoral Music*, 7 (August–September 1983) 16.

PART II

WHO'S HERE?

3

Guests and Servants

Jesus again in reply spoke to them in parables, saying, "The kingdom of heaven may be likened to a king who gave a wedding feast for his son. He dispatched his servants to summon the invited guests to the feast, but they refused to come. A second time he sent other servants, saying, 'Tell those invited: "Behold, I have prepared my banquet, my calves and fattened cattle are killed, and everything is ready; come to the feast."' Some ignored the invitation and went away, one to his farm, another to his business. The rest laid hold of his servants, mistreated them, and killed them. The king was enraged and sent his troops, destroyed those murderers, and burned their city. Then he said to his servants, 'The feast is ready, but those who were invited were not worthy to come. Go out, therefore, into the main roads and invite to the feast whomever you find.' The servants went out into the streets and gathered all they found, bad and good alike, and the hall was filled with guests" (Matt 22:1-10).

An invitation to dinner can come to us in many ways: through the mail; on the phone; electronically; and by word of mouth, as in Jesus' parable of the wedding feast. In this story, a king dispatches his servants (probably with no excessive politeness on his part) to summon previously invited guests to his son's wedding banquet. Apparently people in those days didn't have calendars, appointments secretaries, or pocket PCs to keep them running on schedule. But the servants received unexpected RSVPs: "I *refuse* to come, if you please. . . ."

The king was not pleased at all. "There are some things," he thought, "that just can't—well, *shouldn't*—be missed . . . like the juicy strawberries from my garden (topped with cream!) . . . and the beautiful flowers . . . and the band of musicians that is the finest! What a splendid wedding feast it will be!"

So, the king concluded, "Maybe my servants hadn't combed their hair or shined their sandals or chewed a mint leaf after their garlicky lunch." The king thought he had better send a second set of servants, and so he did.

These servants excitedly told the invited guests: "The dinner is prepared! Everything is now ready! Come to the feast! *Please* come!" Back at the palace, the king was ready, the waiters were ready, the dinner was ready—but the invited guests were not ready to come. "Some ignored the invitation and went away, one to his farm, another to his business. The rest laid hold of his servants, mistreated them, and killed them" (Matt 22:5-6)—a real example of overreacting! But since the guests wouldn't come to visit the king, he sent still other servants—his army—to visit terrible vengeance on them. Perhaps the invited guests never had time to get their important business done . . . .

The feast was still ready, however, despite the empty places at the table and the empty feeling in the king's heart. So he ordered his servants to round up everyone they could find along highways and byways to fill the banquet hall. "Why should everything go to waste?" he asked. The tired servants set out to accomplish their task, knowing that their already long day would be even longer before they blew out the oil lamps. "And the hall was filled with guests" (Matt 22:10).

The Invitation

Jesus, God's chosen Servant, more often called his followers to be servants than guests (see Mark 10:35-45; Luke 12:35-48; Luke 17:7-10). As the evangelist Luke reports (14:7-11), Jesus knew from personal observation that guests can succumb to the temptation to seek extra comfort, honor, and attention. A good servant, however, has no right to expect any of these things. Servants at a banquet are there to serve others, not themselves; Jesus came to serve others, not to be served. It cannot be any different for liturgical ministers who would serve in his name.

Every follower of Jesus is called to serve God and neighbor, yet some are called to be special servants at the Eucharist. They are among their fellow worshipers as those who serve the rest. At the Eucharist, just as at Thanksgiving dinner, some members of the family accept the responsibility of preparing the meal and serving it to the other members of the family. *All* are family, but some are servants and others are guests for that occasion. Similarly, the Eucharist unites the worshipers in the festive meal of God's family, but some worshipers help express that unity through their service to others.

Thus, while servants at the Eucharist never lose sight of their oneness with the priest celebrant as he serves the assembly in its worship,
they never lose sight either of their oneness with their fellow worshipers. "All special ministers are, above all, members of the assembly.
They must know this and show it. They have got to accept this identity. Failure to do so renders their ministry useless and sterile. Nobody
can minister from the outside"[12]—and *inside* is where our baptism
places all of us.

Delight in belonging to God's family assembled for worship is what
gives oneness to the tasks of extending hospitality, proclaiming the
Scriptures, leading the singing, and giving Communion, as well as any
special or unusual demands that may arise, like getting up to light the
candles or turn on the lights or microphone when no one else does, or
getting a book or vessel that is needed, or helping Missy find the Teddy
bear that she lost under the pew. Everything must say to those being
served: "All is now ready! Come to the feast! Come, let us worship the
Lord!" Those whose service is clothing fellow servants and the worship space in festive attire must make the same invitation—liturgical
environment and art should make worshipers eager for the feast and
draw them into the celebration. "Come to the feast!" is an invitation
that comes in many ways, from many servants, during a good liturgy.

"Lift up my heart?"

Yet the invited guests in Jesus' parable showed no eagerness to be
part of the wedding feast, although the servants' invitation was loud
and clear; and they took out their anger and frustration on the servants. Even if these guests had accepted the invitation, they might
have found it very difficult to be part of the celebration. Apparently
they were weighed down by lots of cares and concerns, by a variety of
burdens that would have made the task of the servants at the banquet
even more difficult.

Those who are invited to the liturgy also carry such burdens, as
composer Leonard Bernstein's *Mass: A Theatre Piece for Singers, Players
and Dancers* shows us. *Mass* presents a Celebrant gathering his people
around him for a celebration of the Eucharist. As the Mass progresses,
a deep alienation between the Celebrant and the worshipers becomes

---

[12] Eugene Walsh, *Giving Life: The Ministry of the Parish Sunday Assembly* (Old Hickory, Tenn.: Pastoral Arts Associates of North America, 1982) 11b–12a.

terrifyingly apparent. At the *Confiteor,* the people refuse to offer genuine repentance or seek forgiveness; at the *Gloria,* they mock the "glorious living" that they experience in daily life; at the *Credo,* they express their doubts and disbelief; at the Offertory, they make the bread and wine the objects of a primitive dance.

The tension between the Celebrant and the worshipers becomes most acute at the *Agnus Dei.* In response to their ever more insistent demands, *"Dona nobis PACEM,"* the Celebrant can only offer them *panem,* the bread of life. In utter desperation the Celebrant hurls the consecrated bread and wine to the floor and temporarily loses his mind: "How easily things get broken. . . . I mean, it's *supposed* to be blood . . . I mean, it *is* blood . . . His . . . It was . . . How easily things get broken . . . What are you staring at? Haven't you ever seen an accident before?"[13] The Celebrant's shocking irreverence toward the Body and Blood of Christ only mirrors the daily irreverence shown and suffered by the living members of the Body of Christ around him.

This "accident" brings the worshipers back to their senses. The Lord's Body broken for them, his Blood poured out in their midst, is one with their own brokenness and emptiness. Only now can they receive and share a healing spirit of love for God and for each other. They turn to each other with a tender gesture of reconciliation; the Celebrant rejoins the members of his congregation, who have learned that their faith is greater than their doubt, that their trust is greater than their fear. By the words, music, and gestures of their communal worship, they have learned that love—as a popular and easy slogan—will never solve their problems; but love—sincerely welcomed as a gift from God and celebrated in the assembly—can triumph over hate and doubt. What they have done with and for each other proves true the words of liturgical theologian Odo Casel: the liturgy "is in itself a stream flowing from God's great goodness; it does not merely teach, it leads to love."[14]

---

[13] Libretto of Leonard Bernstein's *Mass: A Theatre Piece for Singers, Players and Dancers* (New York: Amberson Enterprises, Inc., Publisher: G. Schirmer, Inc., Sole Agent, n.d.) 23.

[14] Odo Casel, *The Mystery of Christian Worship,* Burkhard Neunheuser, ed. (Westminster, Md.: Newman Press, 1962) 93.

Heroes Wanted

Bernstein's *Mass* testifies that the task of liturgical servants is not always an easy one. Daniel Berrigan explains why: "According to a liturgical view of life, the world . . . is in the breach; the Christian for whom liturgy is a living and life-giving force enters this breach and, as far as can be done, works to close it."[15] As they assemble for liturgy, those who serve and those who are served cannot leave unsettling cares and concerns in their parked cars or in the cloakroom; adults will (and must) carry them into the worship space just as surely as Missy carries her Teddy bear.

Those who gather for the feast do not pretend that there is no evil or painful side of life, or that they can't see it, hear it, or feel it; rather, they affirm the basic goodness of the world God has given them while not ignoring the evil that threatens them. The "grace" of the Eucharist will not magically remove all questions and doubts, just as it will not magically produce all answers and total faith. The "grace" of the Eucharist enables worshipers to pass over the cracks in human life by affirming that God's immeasurable love is restoring the world to wholeness—but not without their efforts to bring that love to others.

Thus, liturgical servants try to deepen the faith and love of all the worshipers, working to close the chasms of life through the beauty of artistic expression, the Word proclaimed, the voice lifted up in song, the music performed as prayer, the holy gifts shared in love, the words and gestures of welcome and farewell for honored guests.

"Here is the hospitality which forever indicates heroes," as poet Walt Whitman declares. Clearly, "Come to the feast!" is no easy invitation: it requires those who serve the assembly by their holy words and actions to present the nourishing fare that *is* Jesus Christ in Word and sacrament, and not something that merely pleases aesthetic sensibilities or flatters egos (such self-seeking has no place in a good servant). How they enflesh heroic, humble, and responsible service after the example of Jesus Christ helps determine how well or poorly the assembly enfleshes faith in his saving words and deeds.

Truly, the assembly is like the wedding banquet in Jesus' parable—people in varying states of preparedness (physical, emotional, and spiritual) are ushered into the feast. In such a gathering, those who are

---

[15] Daniel Berrigan, *They Call Us Dead Men* (New York: Macmillan, 1962) 157.

burdened under the weight of daily living find hope: "The truest liturgical assembly is that which receives this ordinary people in order to raise them above their hum-drum existence."[16] Such were the people with whom Jesus sat down to table during his earthly life; such are those with whom he now shares the feast in God's reign; such are those to whom the invitation is addressed: "Come to the feast!"

"As special ways of living out the baptismal life of faith," liturgical ministries "demand a renewal of faith in view of the new charge given by the community to the individual. These moments of personal dedication demand reflection, prayer, and discernment so that the decisions to be made may be truly responsive to God's call."[17] The reflection, prayer, and discernment that mark the beginning of such ministry must endure throughout it, even though routine, weariness, and apathy may beset and besiege. Only then can those who serve the assembly at the Eucharist—in every word and action of service offered—invite worshipers to say and mean these words: "It is right to give God thanks and praise." Only then can the priest celebrant proclaim the great Eucharistic Prayer in the name of all, praising God for the divine goodness and victory even in the face of war, family difficulties, unemployment, illness, and death. Such is the message of Bernstein's *Mass*, whose composer has said: "The intention of *Mass* is to communicate as directly and universally as I can a reaffirmation of faith."[18] Liturgical ministers commit themselves to helping the members of the assembly reaffirm their faith as completely as they can—both for themselves and for those they serve.

According to Meister Eckhart, a fourteenth-century mystic, "God does not work in all hearts alike, but according to the preparation and sensitivity he finds in each." The nourishment offered at God's sacramental banquet is infinite—Christ's immeasurable love for us insures that. Yet, we can take away from the feast only what we are prepared to receive; and we help each other to receive God's infinite gifts in the

---

[16] Aimé-Georges Martimort, "L'assembleé liturgique," *La Maison-Dieu*, 20 (1949) 158–59. My trans.

[17] Bishops' Committee on the Liturgy, *Christian Commitment* (Washington, D.C.: United States Catholic Conference, 1978) n.p.

[18] Bernstein, quoted in Paul Hume, "'A Reaffirmation of Faith'", in the souvenir program for Bernstein's *Mass: A Theatre Piece for Singers, Players and Dancers* (Washington, D.C.: The John F. Kennedy Center for the Performing Arts, n.d.) 10.

Eucharist by living our lives with each other graciously and by worshiping together reverently.

Love is never snobbish, never rude, says St. Paul (1 Cor 13:4-5). Irreverence—toward things and especially toward fellow members of the Body of Christ—robs the invitation, "Come to the feast!" of its sincerity and spoils the banquet for both guests and servants. The worshipers in Bernstein's *Mass* had to recognize and reject their negative attitudes toward life before they could open their hearts to God and to each other; only then could they share the feast of God's love together. In the face of whatever cheapens or destroys human life, everyone must embody reverence for God's assembled guests with transparent conviction. When this happens, the Holy Spirit reveals what the reign of God looks, sounds, and feels like through the invitation: "Come to the feast!"

"Thou, of souls the sweetest guest!"

The most welcome and indispensable guest at every liturgy is the Holy Spirit, who animates all effective planning and service. In the liturgy, the Spirit gathers the worshipers together and helps them to reaffirm their faith through words, music, and gestures. Liturgical ministers must discern and follow the Spirit's lead, always trying to insure that it is the Gospel of Christ, and not some other message, that is announced in all planning and service. Then Christ will be powerfully present in the midst of his people at prayer, and they will be powerfully present to him as a people praying in his name.

The Spirit chooses to use our hearts, hands, and voices to form the Body of Christ at worship. "Every quality, common or extraordinary, placed at the service of others through the impulse of the Spirit, is a charism. Singing and organization, graciousness and any other skill useful for animating the feast is a charism."[19] Yet in spite of the Spirit's constant animating of the liturgy, liturgical celebrations will continue to leave many worshipers (even the ministers who worked longest and hardest on them) feeling a little empty, no matter how appealing the "packaging" may be. Liturgical enthusiasm or "peak experiences" can never completely remove the anxiety and restlessness that are found in each worshiper in varying degrees.

---

[19] Juan Mateos, *Beyond Conventional Christianity,* Kathleen England, trans. (Manila: East Asian Pastoral Institute, 1974) 322.

When I served as pastor, I had a tiny bulletin board in the sacristy. It was a handy place to post reminders to myself, but also an occasional meditation or two. One of my favorites is this one from the rite of ordination to the priesthood: "Accept from the holy people of God the gifts to be offered to God. Know what you are doing, and imitate the mystery you celebrate: Model your life on the mystery of the Lord's cross." The last line is the one that grabs me: "Model your life on the mystery of the Lord's *cross.*" Not the mystery of the Lord's birth, or his resurrection, or another of the mysteries of the Rosary, but on the mystery of his *cross.* Why the *cross?*

The answer is that our life, as our ministry, draws its power for good from the mystery of the Lord's self-sacrifice unto death. We need to model both our life and our ministry on the mystery of the Lord's cross, a mystery of self-sacrificing love. Liturgical ministry comprises much spiritual joy, but also lots of routine and schedule conflicts and thankless service. Here is the cross, some share in it that you accept in your ministry.

Servants must expect to participate a bit differently from guests, because servants have accepted a special responsibility to represent the Lord Jesus, whose self-giving must be the pattern for their own. Also, the servants have been part of the liturgy from the first moments of its preparation, often long before the actual celebration begins (every liturgy committee knows that it must live the liturgical seasons months before the rest of the parish does). Like careful cooks, they taste the goodness of the feast in advance, so that they can (and must) welcome everyone with art, words, music, and gestures that say: "Come to the feast!"

Since the Spirit is not stingy, advance participation does not give exclusive ownership of the feast. Love for all God's holy people and holy things must be an unfailing rule. The servants in the Gospel parable probably didn't treat those who finally shared the banquet as second-rate guests (after all, the servants had worked hard to get them there). Worshipers must never be treated as second-rate guests—no matter if they sing a little off-key, or don't move very fast going to Communion, or don't know a purificator from a finger towel, or sit as though they were playing hide-and-seek in the nearly empty church at the early Mass.

It is only by joyfully inviting the guests to the feast that the servants (who are also guests) can enjoy the feast themselves. Accepting this invitation, the assembled guests share the privilege of praising and thanking their God, as well as the duty of serving each other—imperfect as such worship and service are. A fourth-century Church document called *The Apostolic Constitutions* is only being honest when it declares: "We thank you, almighty God, not as we should but as we can."[20] The gracious invitation, "Come to the feast!," ideally helps move the "as we can" of the assembly's worship closer to the "as we should."

---

[20] *Constitutiones Apostolorum*, VIII, 12, 35, quoted in Marcel Metzger, "The Didascalia and the Constitutiones Apostolorum," *The Eucharist of the Early Christians*, Matthew J. O'Connell, trans. (New York: Pueblo Publishing, 1978) 210.

4

In Company with
Angels and Archangels

> You have not approached that which could be touched and a blazing fire
> and gloomy darkness and storm and a trumpet blast and a voice speak-
> ing words such that those who heard begged that no message be further
> addressed to them. [. . .] No, you have approached Mount Zion and
> the city of the living God, the heavenly Jerusalem, and countless angels
> in festal gathering, and the assembly of the firstborn enrolled in heaven,
> and God the judge of all, and the spirits of the just made perfect, and
> Jesus, the mediator of a new covenant, and the sprinkled blood that
> speaks more eloquently than that of Abel (Heb 12:18-19, 22-24).

I believe in lots of things that I do not completely understand, humanly speaking: things that are filled with the mystery of God. Like
electricity, that makes the night bright as day; or music that brings me
to tears; or flowers, God's best poetry; or people who give their love
and encouragement, no matter what.

I believe in angels because I believe that there is divine mystery in
our worship. There is more to our worship than we can see or hear or
touch, humanly speaking. Part of this mystery is that the angels worship *with* us, today and every day.

"We are not alone," declared the poster for the movie *Close Encounters of the Third Kind*. That movie assured us earthlings that we are not
alone because visitors from outer space stop by from time to time. But
the Bible gives us greater assurance that we are not alone. We have
come to "the city of the living God, the heavenly Jerusalem, and
countless angels in festal gathering" (Heb. 12:22). We are not alone as
we gather to perform one of our greatest human privileges and duties:
our worship of almighty God. We are not alone as we worship, for in
our festal gathering every Sunday we experience close encounters of

the *angelic* kind—if we have eyes to see and ears to hear their mysterious presence in our worship.

The Church believes that its worship on earth blends with the worship of the angels and saints in heaven. Or, to put this another way, the angels become participating members of every earthly congregation as it worships—though it must be admitted that angels are very poor contributors to the collection. But how greatly they delight in our worship of God, for how greatly they delight in the God whom we worship! They delight in our worship because they know it is something *grand:* they know that our worship is our foretaste of God's eternal feast of victory to come, after Satan and all God's enemies are finally overthrown. That's something worth celebrating right now, and the angels wouldn't miss being part of it. That's why they join us earthlings in our worship, for here we celebrate *now* the life we hope to share with them forever.

Saint Benedict knew that we are not alone as we worship. He knew that we are in the best of company—the holy angels—and so our conduct at worship should be the best. Thus he tells his monks in his Rule: "We must always remember . . . what the Prophet says: . . . *In the presence of the angels I will sing to you* (Ps 137[138]:1). Let us consider then, how we ought to behave in the presence of God and his angels, and let us stand to sing the psalms in such a way that our minds are in harmony with our voices."[21] Some monasteries of former times tried to imitate the angels' unceasing prayer by organizing their monks into shifts, who then sent public prayer aloft twenty-four hours a day.

Saint Benedict's point is not that we should be in church all the time, but that our minds should be in harmony with our voices when we worship. Such harmony of mind and voice can be difficult for us, yet such is the angels' unceasing, effortless offering of praise to almighty God. The angels are most eager to do as the psalmist tells them: "Bless the Lord, all you angels, mighty in strength and attentive, obedient to every command. Bless the Lord, all you hosts, ministers who do God's will" (Ps 103:20-21). The angels are eager to bless God unceasingly, as the fourth Roman Eucharistic Prayer declares: "Countless hosts of angels stand before you to do your will; they look upon your splendor and praise you, night and day."

---

[21] *RB 1980: The Rule of St. Benedict in English,* Timothy Fry, O.S.B., et al., eds. (Collegeville: Liturgical Press, 1982), ch. 19, 47.

Such language should lead us earthlings to make a humble admission: we are only beginners, mere apprentices, in the offering of divine praise. The angels have the edge. After all, God made us mortals only a little less than the angels—but *less,* nonetheless. It is good for us to remember that there exist angelic beings who are just a bit better than we are in the worship—the divine service—that we share with them as co-ministers. The angels *never* tire of praising God. They *never* cease protecting God's holy people, especially the least ones. They *never* grow weary of doing good, of doing God's will.

But how often *we* do! How weary we can get as we prepare for worship week after week: preparing to preach the homily or read the lessons, rehearsing the music, assisting at the altar, ministering Communion, making sure that everyone and everything is in good order, and, last but not least, rounding up the family, toys and all, for the trek to church. Are there not times when we need all the help we can get to worship well, including the help of the angels? Maybe that's why God sent the angel host to the sleepy shepherds on the first Christmas Eve: God wanted to get them to the crib on time (and how could they possibly sleep after all that angelic merry-making?).

Must we not draw some encouragement from the thought that there are living beings who have spent the near-eternity since their creation praising God for the divine goodness and glory, and who never get tired of doing so? Doesn't the example of the angels encourage us to worship God as willingly, faithfully, and joyfully as they do?

PART III

WHAT HAPPENS?

5

The Waiting Lord

Then the angel of the LORD came and sat under the terebinth in Ophrah that belonged to Joash the Abiezrite. While his son Gideon was beating out wheat in the wine press to save it from the Midianites, the angel of the LORD appeared to him and said, "The LORD is with you, O champion!" "My LORD," Gideon said to him, "if the LORD is with us, why has all this happened to us? Where are his wondrous deeds of which our fathers told us when they said, 'Did not the LORD bring us up from Egypt?' For now the LORD has abandoned us and has delivered us into the power of Midian." The LORD turned to him and said, "Go with the strength you have and save Israel from the power of Midian. It is I who send you." But he answered him, "Please, my lord, how can I save Israel? My family is the meanest in Manasseh, and I am the most insignificant in my father's house." "I shall be with you," the LORD said to him, "and you will cut down Midian to the last man." He answered him, "If I find favor with you, give me a sign that you are speaking with me. Do not depart from here, I pray you, until I come back to you and bring out my offering and set it before you." He answered, "I will await your return."

So Gideon went off and prepared a kid and an ephah of flour in the form of unleavened cakes. Putting the meat in a basket and the broth in a pot, he brought them out to him under the terebinth and presented them. The angel of God said to him, "Take the meat and unleavened cakes and lay them on this rock; then pour out the broth." When he had done so, the angel of the LORD stretched out the tip of the staff he held, and touched the meat and unleavened cakes. Thereupon a fire came up from the rock which consumed the meat and unleavened cakes, and the angel of the LORD disappeared from sight. Gideon, now aware that it had been the angel of the LORD, said, "Alas, Lord, GOD, that I have seen the angel of the LORD face to face!" The LORD answered him, "Be calm, do not fear. You shall not die." So Gideon built there an altar to the LORD and called it Yahweh-shalom (Judg 6:11-24).

I was seated comfortably in the presider's chair as the elderly Sister at the convent infirmary Eucharist took up the book and began to read. Soon her mistake was evident, at least to me: she was reading the first lesson for Year I (Judg 6:11-24) instead of that for Year II (Ezek 28:1-10). I didn't have the heart to stop her (and besides, I was not going to preach on the first lesson anyway). Thus we got to hear the story of Gideon's commissioning by the angel of the Lord instead of the Lord's verbal barrage against the prince of Tyre. It was just as well, for this serendipitous mistake (or providence) gave me an insight into liturgical ministry—the Lord waits while we prepare ourselves for service to God and God's people.

In the narrative from the book of Judges, Gideon encounters the apparently incognito "angel of the LORD" (really the biblical writer's way of designating the LORD). The angel has some surprising news for Gideon: he is to be an instrument of deliverance for his people, who are sorely oppressed by the Midianites. Gideon realizes that this won't be easy, and so he protests his insignificance and incompetence for such a task. But to really decide the matter, Gideon seeks a sign of his election by God and a proof of God's favor in this undertaking. And he begins how any good Israelite would: with an act of worship. Gideon believes that the Lord's acceptance or rejection of a sacrifice will make clear to him what he must do. So Gideon politely asks his companion to wait while he gets everything ready. And the angel politely answers, "I will await your return."

That reply sends Gideon off to hustle and bustle like those who serve up burgers and fries at fast-food restaurants. He hurries to get his offering ready: a kid from the flock and about a bushel (!) of flour shaped into unleavened cakes, and some broth to go with it. A large take-out order!

The angel of the Lord is still waiting when Gideon returns. The angel directs Gideon to lay the meat and unleavened cakes on a rock, and to pour out the broth. When Gideon has carefully done so, the angel touches the offering with the tip of his staff. Presto! Fire consumes Gideon's sacrifice and takes it up to heaven, and the angel vanishes too.

Only now does Gideon realize that his companion was none other than the "angel of the LORD" (remember, this means the LORD). Terror grips Gideon, for he and other Israelites believed that no one was able to survive a face-to-face encounter with the very holiness of God. But the Lord calms Gideon's fears and assures him that he will not die.

Gideon again responds with an act of worship. He builds an altar to the Lord and calls it "Yhwh-shalom." "Yes, the Lord truly is peace," Gideon must have thought as he remembered his offering and the altar which now memorialized it.

The scriptural narrative does not tell us how Gideon felt while he was preparing his offering. Perhaps he said to himself: "I must make everything just right. . . . It's for the Lord!" Gideon is one in spirit with liturgical ministers who work hard to offer God the best of their talents—the best welcoming, reading, presiding, assisting, preaching, music-making. All we do within the liturgy is for the Lord and the Lord's people. The liturgy places us in the best of company—the holy angels and saints, our co-worshipers—and so our conduct within the liturgy should be the best. And like Gideon, we discover that much depends on our hard work and generous offering, for our words and gestures reveal the Lord's presence in the worshiping assembly.

Neither does the scriptural narrative tell us how the angel of the Lord felt about waiting for Gideon to prepare his offering. But the Lord knows that we mortals usually need a little time to accomplish almost everything we do, and lots of time for the really important things. So the angel of the Lord must have waited patiently for Gideon to prepare and return with his offering.

The Lord awaits the offering of liturgical ministers, too. The Lord waits while they prepare to offer themselves and their talents as spiritual worship pleasing to God within the liturgy. The Lord waits for all of us to complete our preparation for worship, both our remote preparation (like putting on our Sunday best) and our immediate preparation (like praying before the liturgy begins). The Lord waits for us to get our cakes baked and our meat prepared—our offerings of welcoming, making music, presiding, assisting, reading the Scripture lessons, chanting the responsorial psalm, preaching the homily, ministering Communion, participating fully in the liturgy. The Lord waits for us to get our music selected, our leaflets printed, our readings practiced, our bread baked and our wine poured out, our worship spaces prepared, our songs rehearsed, our instruments tuned, our assemblies gathered, *ourselves* ready for service. The Lord waits while we prepare the externals of worship (people, places, and things) in the hope that thereby we will be prepared internally for worship.

We can profit from some mid-fifteenth century words addressed to the Bridgettine nuns of Syon Abbey: "Though it be not in our power to have devotion at our will, for it is the free gift of God, yet it is in our power by grace to do that which is in us to dispose us to devotion. And the great courtesy of our merciful Lord is freely to give the gifts of grace and devotion to them that faithfully dispose themselves thereto. And if he give them not to our feeling he gives them to our greatest profit, if the default be not in us."[22] The Lord helps you to prepare a spiritual sacrifice of devotion and lay it down first of all in your own heart. It is there that you must first make your offering to God; it is there that you must first build an altar to the Lord if the one in church truly is to receive your offering in union with Christ's. Our hearts must truly bear the sacred name, "Yahweh-shalom," "The Lord is peace," if we are to embody the peace of the Lord in our worship and share it with others. A rubric of the Byzantine Rite reminds the priest who is about to celebrate the Eucharist that he must be reconciled with all people and have nothing against anyone. Such a reminder is fitting for all who encounter the Lord's holiness as they minister at the Lord's table. If your heart is thus prepared, you have the Lord's promise that your hands and voice also will be ready for service to God and God's people.

The Lord patiently awaits our carefully prepared yet often less-than-perfect offerings. The Lord graciously touches our offerings of material goods and human talent with a staff during the liturgy and transforms them into something grand, a sacrifice that rises up to heaven. Truly the Lord *must* enkindle our greater and lesser gifts with the Spirit's flame if they are to be acceptable in God's sight. The Lord must touch our preparation for liturgical ministry if we are to find the right words to say, prayers to pray, notes to play, and art to display within the assembly. But the Lord doesn't mind waiting while we prepare ourselves and our gifts. The Lord is used to waiting upon liturgical ministers, for the Lord has been doing so for centuries:

- The Lord waited while the Levites at the Temple in Jerusalem slaughtered the unblemished animals for sacrifice and while the priests laid them on the altar's flames to the accompaniment of harping and psalm singing.
- The Lord waited while the apostles prepared the paschal lamb and set the festive table for the last Passover meal that Jesus would celebrate with them.

[22] *The Myroure of oure Ladye,* John Henry Blunt, ed. (Early English Text Society, XIX; London: N. Trubner, 1873) 21. I have modernized the English of the text somewhat.

- The Lord waited while the early Christians processed to the altars in the Roman basilicas, each carrying the homemade bread and wine which would become the sacred feast shared by all.
- The Lord waited while nearly illiterate Carolingian priests fumbled their way through the intricacies of the new Roman liturgical books, with maybe only an adolescent acolyte to help them through the daily services.
- The Lord waited while early medieval bishops sent their liturgy staffs to rummage in Rome's Lateran archives and copy out texts for use back home, thus giving them and us a wealth of treasured prayers and blessings.
- The Lord waited while medieval monks and nuns marked and prepared their Scripture readings for Mass and Office, in spite of sometimes poor copies and bad lighting.
- The Lord waited while J. S. Bach, after a full morning at church, hurried through Sunday dinner and immediately began work on the cantata that needed to be written, printed, and rehearsed for the following Sunday.
- The Lord waited while early twentieth century choirs practiced the *Asperges me,* chant Mass VIII, and *Panis Angelicus.*
- The Lord waited while Jewish prisoners in the concentration camps uncovered their tiny silver menorahs and prepared to let the Hanukkah lights dispel the darkness within and without.
- The Lord waited while Sister trained the altar servers for the newly restored Easter Vigil in the 1950s, although she knew full well that on the Great Night nobody would know where to stand and everybody would stand where nobody was supposed to.
- The Lord waited while priests and congregations learned to pray the vernacular texts of the renewed liturgy after the Second Vatican Council.

Truly the Lord waits while *we* prepare to offer our liturgical service:

- The Lord waits while sacristans arrange flowers, lay out books and vestments, test microphones, and make sure that everything is ready.
- The Lord waits while ministers of music prepare to celebrate the reign of God in hymns and melodies of the Spirit's making.
- The Lord waits while lectors prepare to bring the Word of God to life on their lips and in our hearts.

- The Lord waits while ministers of hospitality prepare to welcome God's honored guests to the festal gathering where all are one in Christ Jesus.
- The Lord waits while priests and deacons prepare to serve the assembly at the tables of the Lord's Word and the Lord's Supper.
- The Lord waits while altar servers prepare to reflect in their pleasing appearance and gracious actions the ministry of angels around God's throne.
- The Lord waits while extraordinary ministers of Holy Communion prepare to give the Eucharist to their sisters and brothers within the assembly, and while they carry it to those absent members whom the assembly embraces through their ministry.

The Lord waits while we prepare to exercise our ministry—the ministry of the *whole* people. Preparation *itself* is sacred, for it serves to deepen devotion and reverence. It reminds us that we are one in calling and spirit with worshipers in all times and places: in the ancient house churches of downtown Corinth and Ephesus; in the ancient basilicas of Rome and Constantinople; in the great cathedrals and monastic churches of medieval Europe; in the log chapels of colonial America; in the adobe mission churches of the Spanish Southwest; in the new churches of Africa and Asia; in the ethnic churches of urban neighborhoods and rural areas; in the space where your parish family is truly "at home" as it worships together. Here the Lord touches the offerings of the assembly and the ministry of those who serve it, transforming them by the flames of divine love into an acceptable sacrifice.

6

Changing Water into Wine

On the third day there was a wedding at Cana in Galilee, and the mother of Jesus was there. Jesus and his disciples were also invited to the wedding. When the wine ran short, the mother of Jesus said to him, "They have no wine." [And] Jesus said to her, "Woman, how does your concern affect me? My hour has not yet come." His mother said to the servers, "Do whatever he tells you." Now there were six stone water jars there for Jewish ceremonial washings, each holding twenty to thirty gallons. Jesus told them, "Fill the jars with water." So they filled them to the brim. Then he told them, "Draw some out now and take it to the headwaiter." So they took it. And when the headwaiter tasted the water that had become wine, without knowing where it came from (although the servers who had drawn the water knew), the headwaiter called the bridegroom and said to him, "Everyone serves good wine first, and then when people have drunk freely, an inferior one; but you have kept the good wine until now." Jesus did this as the beginning of his signs in Cana in Galilee and so revealed his glory, and his disciples began to believe in him (John 2:1-11).

Sometimes I wish I could design greeting cards; the people who do seem so clever and creative, and so does their work. Take the card, for example, that portrays this Gospel story. One of the waiters at the wedding at Cana grandly announces: "Here's a better vintage that Jesus just provided." A thirsty guest reaches for a goblet with wine splashing out and says: "I'll try it." And when you open the card: "May God make this year better than any that's gone before. Happy Birthday!"

What would it have been like to taste the marvelous vintage that Jesus provided to spare the newlyweds a social catastrophe?

Wonders of wonders, God works a greater miracle for us, right here and now. God gives us an exquisite wine that we can't buy in any store, but God gives it to us here for free—the liturgy we celebrate. God transforms our human words, songs, and gestures into something that pleases our God and lifts our spirits. In the liturgy we celebrate, our human gifts are transformed by God's power into a most powerful and refreshing wine. In the liturgy, God transforms our gifts of bread and wine into the Body and Blood of God's Son, but God also changes our lives into a living sacrifice of praise.

How does God do this? Through the ministry of generous women and men who assist the assembly in its worship, Sunday after Sunday and throughout the week, God transforms human actions into something that gladdens our hearts as nothing else can. This is the wine of which St. Paul said: "Be filled with the Spirit, addressing one another [in] psalms and hymns and spiritual songs" (Eph 5:18-19a). For the Holy Spirit, who transforms the bread and wine into the Body and Blood of Christ, transforms us into the members of his Body. And as we worship, the human elements of our worship—our human words and actions—become divine praise.

But before this transformation can happen, we need to do what the waiters did at the wedding at Cana. They needed to draw the water as Jesus told them. And so do we need to fill ourselves with a certain "water": love for the Word of God we hear in church and read at home; commitment to communal prayer in church and at home; looking at the material objects and outward signs of our worship and seeing God working through them for our salvation. Such is the preparation for God's transforming action in the liturgy that results in our full, conscious, and active participation. When we are filled to our spiritual brim with such preparation for worship, the wine that God produces in our liturgy will be rich indeed.

This is how Jesus Christ satisfies our thirst for God's life and love— he gives us the wine of the liturgy to savor and enjoy. This is how Jesus Christ gives us now a foretaste of the wine that God will serve on the final day, when the eternal feast of life and love will begin and never end.

But while we wait for that grand celebration, why not enjoy each liturgy, right here and right now? Take your glass and let God fill it with the overflowing love offered to us in our worship.

PART IV

WHO DO WE BECOME?

7

The Ministry Quilt

I urge you therefore, brothers [and sisters], by the mercies of God, to offer your bodies as a living sacrifice, holy and pleasing to God, your spiritual worship. Do not conform yourselves to this age but be transformed by the renewal of your mind, that you may discern what is the will of God, what is good and pleasing and perfect (Rom 12:1-2).

There are different kinds of spiritual gifts but the same Spirit; there are different forms of service but the same Lord; there are different workings but the same God who produces all of them in everyone. To each individual the manifestation of the Spirit is given for some benefit (1 Cor 12:4-7).

Autumn turning into winter. The crops are in, weighed, counted, sold, or stored up. We have emptied out the flower boxes and planters, split the last pieces of firewood, counted and cleaned the blankets. And the quilts.

With the coming of cold weather, my body and mind turn to quilts. I replace my light-weight and light-colored summer bedspread with the heavier and darker quilt that I bought decades ago. It is full of $3\frac{1}{2}$ inch squares in shades of my favorite color: brown, brown, and more brown.

The challenge in quilt-making, so I'm told, is this: creating a unity from different patches while respecting diversity and complementarity. Truly every quilt, and every life, begins with scattered pieces before its overall beauty emerges. And this is true of the liturgy as well.

What if we were to create a quilt to celebrate liturgical ministry during the past century? What would it look like? What would we depict there?

Let's start around the year 1903, when Orville and Wilbur Wright were getting airborne, and Pope Pius X issued his important letter on sacred music. What liturgical ministers would we have at Mass at the beginning of the twentieth century?

The priest, of course, plus, at solemn High Mass, two other priests masquerading as deacon and subdeacon; lots of altar boys (no girls) in freshly pressed cassocks and surplices; and ushers (there have always been ushers, it seems—maybe even at the Last Supper). The deacon and subdeacon didn't really serve the assembly, but they added some external solemnity and more color through more Mass vestments. For centuries the Mass servers had taken over the responses and prayers that had been the assembly's in earlier times; these were restored to the assembly, in Latin, in the "dialogue Mass" of the 1950s, and in the vernacular after the Second Vatican Council. So our quilt square for the year 1903 would have a heavily clerical pattern: lots of lacey surplices and fiddleback vestments and such. And completely male.

Jump to 1968, just three years after Vatican II ended. Already the picture of ministry at Mass is quite different. Commentators are giving explanations of the parts of the Mass; laypersons, women and men, are proclaiming the Scripture readings in their own language and announcing the intentions of the general intercessions; of course the servers and ushers are still there. So our quilt square from the late 1960s would have to represent this necessary group of lectors proclaiming God's Word to God's people.

Now jump to 1974, one year after laypersons were permitted to minister Holy Communion at Mass and outside of Mass. This ministry was established not just to assist the priest, though that it does. Extraordinary ministers of Holy Communion help to unify the assembly's receiving Christ the Lord by their service, so that it doesn't seem an eternity between the communion of the first communicant and the last. Our ministry quilt square needs to represent extraordinary ministers of Holy Communion. And also deacons, especially permanent deacons. Since Vatican II, the priest and the deacon at the Eucharist are like the captain and first-officer of the liturgy, assisting us in what we hope will be a smooth liturgical flight. So deacons will need to be represented on our quilt square. And of course ushers, who in a sense are flight attendants in our liturgies who welcome us and care for our needs.

What about choirs and musicians? Weren't they part of the Mass in the year 1903 and in subsequent years? Yes. But early in the last century, no one thought of music-making as a *ministry*. Again, it was something that added splendor and solemnity to the Mass, but wasn't all that necessary. Today music is as expected at the Eucharist as light and heat in the building, and rightly so. We have come to understand that making music, expressing our prayer musically in the sacramental rites and worship of the Church, is a most basic and most important ministry.

So what do we learn from our ministry quilt squares throughout the past century? More and more laypersons have accepted more and more roles of service within the liturgy. Liturgy in the spirit of Vatican II is the coordinated action of different ministries—ushers/greeters, musicians, priest, deacon, readers, servers, extraordinary ministers of Holy Communion, and, indeed, the entire assembly. The sanctuary, which used to be mostly "clergy-only" territory, has become a place where clergy and laypersons together serve this primary liturgical minister, the gathered people of God.

The renewal of various specific liturgical ministries exercised by laypersons should promote the liturgy's most important ministry, the assembly's. All special ministries exist to serve the principal liturgical minister, the assembly. Why is the assembly the primary liturgical minister? Because the assembly is one with Jesus Christ, the supreme liturgist, the supreme liturgical minister before God and with us. The assembly becomes a body that lives, the Body of Christ. The selfless service of liturgical ministers helps all the worshipers turn the "I" of self into the "we" of the assembly; thus "Christ is all and in all" (Col 3:11), the unity of our ministry quilt.

The essence of liturgy is each person's contribution of presence and participation offered to all, so that the gifts of each may enrich all. In celebrating liturgy, as in making a quilt, the work of each individual is done for the good of a greater whole. That whole, that community, is formed by God so that it may help to reform the world according to God's plan. Then God's love can reside there and be at home, until we wrap ourselves in the quilt of God's everlasting life and love.

Sometimes I wonder if people really hear the prayers that the priest prays in their name at Mass, like the opening prayer, or like this prayer over the gifts for the Twenty-Fourth Sunday in Ordinary Time:

> Lord,
> hear the prayers of your people
> and receive our gifts.
> May the worship of each one here
> bring salvation to all.
> Grant this through Christ our Lord.

This prayer expresses so clearly what our liturgy, our worship, is: the prayers and gifts of each person offered to God, but also shared among all. And in sharing our prayers and gifts, by God's power and action in Christ, we create something great, something grand, something that is greater and grander than any one person could create.

What kind of prayers do we bring to God? Adoration, repentance, petition, thanksgiving.

What kind of gifts do we bring to God? Money, yes, but mainly our talents and skills—singing in the choir, reading the Scripture lessons, serving at the altar, actively participating as the assembly. Not just the gifts of bread and wine, but our whole lives given to God in company with Jesus Christ. That's an offer God can't refuse, a gift that God delights in!

In a world where service is often cold and impersonal, liturgical ministry is like a quilt: not to lull people to sleep, but to be a warm reassurance of God's care for each of us, the little no less than the great. God's "little ones" are those who put their trust in God, because that is the real source of their hope. God's care comes to everyone at the Eucharist, but it comes to them through our ministry, a very human ministry that needs divine purpose and power. There may be tedium and joy in our ministry; but here also is the stuff of our personal ministry quilt square. And the invisible thread holding every minister's experiences together and uniting them to every other minister's are the Gospel words of Jesus: "For the Son of Man did not come to be served but to serve and to give his life as a ransom for many" (Mark 10:45).

8

Chosen Race, Royal Priesthood, Holy People

Come to him, a living stone, rejected by human beings but chosen and precious in the sight of God, and, like living stones, let yourselves be built into a spiritual house to be a holy priesthood to offer spiritual sacrifices acceptable to God through Jesus Christ. [. . .] [Y]ou are "a chosen race, a royal priesthood, a holy nation, a people of his own, so that you may announce the praises" of him who called you out of darkness into his wonderful light (1 Pet 2:4-5, 9).

Since the Second Vatican Council my Benedictine Abbey, Saint John's in Collegeville, Minnesota, has prepared participation leaflets for its Sunday Eucharist. Those from the "early years" are marked by unsurpassed creativity. One such leaflet for the Holy Thursday Eucharist unfolds to reveal, on the inside, a large (22½" x 17½") red-and-white checkered "Italian" tablecloth, with thirteen place settings around the four sides. The music for the celebration, in the center of the table, serves as part of that evening's nourishing feast.

While the table arrangements depicted in this leaflet do not conform to those of the last Passover meal that Jesus shared with his disciples, we glimpse here the order and basic equality that must be part of the eucharistic meal that Jesus now shares with us. We are rediscovering the goodness of table fellowship based on the baptismal equality of all who participate, ordained and non-ordained alike.

Baptism makes us all equal, all privileged. When we enter the holy house for worship we must leave at the door whatever our pride makes us hold most dear—our special claims to honor, our personal achievements, our good works. Such pride and self-importance have no place in those who could never earn the priceless gift that God lavishes upon us in the Body and Blood of Christ.

Today some in the Church believe that "lay ministry" is a contradiction in terms. It is sad to hear that some still see the church building as divided into "clerical space" and "lay space" rather than as a unified sacred space made so by the sacred people of God (both ordained and non-ordained) and by their sacred actions in company with Christ.

Blessed be those who promote lay ministry as the expected (not extraordinary) flowering of the commitment made to Christ at baptism and renewed each year at Easter. For all ordained ministers start out in some way as *lay* ministers, whether in official capacities or not. Many clergy celebrate the fact that they received their first and best education in Christian ministry from their parents, relatives, friends, and fellow parishioners, and then came to imitate that ministry in various ways both before and after ordination. Ministry, whether by laypersons or ordained persons, is something we grow into, something we shape ourselves into as it shapes us; ministry is not something that comes ready-made, once for all, at ordination or rite of commissioning. Off-the-rack ministry doesn't exist; it must be tailored to each minister, in particular settings and through diverse experiences. To paraphrase Tertullian in the third century, ministers (both lay and ordained) are made, not born. And they must help make each other into what each needs to be.

Will there be any "going back" in the matter of lay ministry in the Church? Will laypersons be deprived of opportunities that they rightly have become accustomed to? One hopes not, because worshipers' changing liturgical consciousness may just now be catching up with liturgical changes over four decades ago (remember the role-playing children I wrote about in the Introduction). One cannot help being disturbed by nostalgia for a former era when the abundance of clerics made the sanctuary into "clergy only" territory (except for altar boys, church cleaners, and couples on their wedding day), when the liturgical ministry of laypersons was unimagined and hence undesired.

"Lovers of the theatrical may be pleased at the cast of performers in the sanctuary where once the sacred mysteries were action enough,"[23] sarcastically observes a disgruntled layman. But in the centuries when the Mass of the Roman Rite was acquiring its classic shape, a host of

---

[23] John J. Farrell, "The Church that never was," *Homiletic & Pastoral Review* 88 (January 1988) 52.

different ministers celebrating the sacred mysteries in union with the assembly was the rule, not the exception. Their coordinated ministries revealed the sacred mysteries present before them, through them, and in them. Today, the triple focus of the post-Vatican II liturgy (altar, lectern, presider's chair) and the assembly's recovered role as primary liturgical minister, render anyone's exclusive claim to the sanctuary untenable. The cooperation of different yet complementary ministries must become visible everywhere in the worship space, but that cooperation must be found first of all in the hearts of all who minister there, ordained and non-ordained alike. Such is the leadership of worship that is strong enough to defer to other leaders and ministers when necessary. "It is leadership which insists on the full, conscious, and active participation by all in our corporate prayer. It is leadership which studiously avoids word, glance, posture or tone which suggests superiority."[24]

There are some worship spaces that render such superiority nearly impossible. On August 4, 1988, it was my privilege to participate in the patronal feast day celebration at Santo Domingo Pueblo in northern New Mexico. Before the early-morning Mass in the centuries-old mission church, an elderly Indian gentleman named Santiago was busy making final preparations, just as he had for half a century in his role as *sacristán*. After leading me and the other concelebrants in procession to the none-too-spacious sanctuary, he gracefully took the only seat available there—the one next to me—for the rest of the liturgy.

It is true that according to the rubrics, the various ministers (priest, concelebrants, deacon) should have separate seats so as to avoid confusion of roles. Of course, even though Santiago was sitting with the concelebrants, he wasn't dressed like one or acting like one, and thus no confusion could result. But somehow it seemed very proper that Santiago should sit where he did. In a sense, he belonged there more than I did (this was his local church and patronal feast) and, as server, he should have a seat near the altar (and, as I said, there was only one left). But most of all, he was a true "celebrant," just as all the baptized Christians present at that liturgy were, and especially so in his ministry to all of them. The beauty of his service, more than space limitations, made the fact of where he sat irrelevant. Service, not seating, was primary for him.

---

[24] Tim Fitzgerald, "Lectors, Cantors, Presiders: Let Us See Through You," *Liturgy 80* 19 (May–June 1988) 14.

We can never claim a *right* to enter the sanctuary and minister the holy gifts of God to the holy people of God; indeed, even angels would shy away from so exalted a task. During the Eucharistic Prayer, a presiding bishop customarily names himself an "unworthy servant." While the worshipers probably will hold different opinions about his worthiness, there is profound truth in this expression: no one is worthy to claim by *right* the familiar access to God that the liturgy gives us. Through our baptism into Christ, we have received this *privilege*, and all liturgical ministry also is a privilege. This privilege comes as a gift from God in baptism. As the people of God assembled for worship, our roles and responsibilities within the celebration vary, and rightly so. But our baptismal priesthood is the heart of them all. Indeed, our "spiritual life is a continual procession from baptistry to altar,"[25] in the words of my deceased Benedictine confrere, Cloud Meinberg. Herein lies any "right" we might have to share liturgical ministry with the priest. But that "right" is really a privilege given to us by God, not a permission granted to us or an honor bestowed on us by the pastor or anyone else.

Today we expect to find a diversity of ministries within the liturgical assembly in accord with official documents. But what binds these ministries together is not a carefully maintained system of rights and privileges, nor jealously defended areas of liturgical "turf" (*my* sanctuary, *my* turn and place to function, *my* Communion-call circuit). The principle of unity that ought to shape the thinking and acting of liturgical ministers is love expressed in service, "serve one another through love" (Gal 5:13). Love for God and God's holy people must be expressed in unity before, during, and after our worship together. Such is the love that triumphs over all human divisions and inequalities, for it looks away from self to God's gifts and others' needs. The more that we embody such loving service, both within the liturgy and outside it, the easier we will find it to think of ministry in terms of "we" and "ours" instead of "I" and "mine." And then we will "find ourselves in the place just right," wherever we minister.

[25] Cloud H. Meinberg, O.S.B., *An Outline History of Sacred Art* (Collegeville: The University Press, 1959) 252.

PART V

WHAT HAPPENS NEXT?

9

We Have Seen the Lord

Now that very day two of them were going to a village seven miles from Jerusalem called Emmaus, and they were conversing about all the things that had occurred. And it happened that while they were conversing and debating, Jesus himself drew near and walked with them, but their eyes were prevented from recognizing him. He asked them, "What are you discussing as you walk along?" They stopped, looking downcast. One of them, named Cleopas, said to him in reply, "Are you the only visitor to Jerusalem who does not know of the things that have taken place there in these days?" And he replied to them, "What sort of things?" They said to him, "The things that happened to Jesus the Nazarene, who was a prophet mighty in deed and word before God and all the people, how our chief priests and rulers both handed him over to a sentence of death and crucified him. But we were hoping that he would be the one to redeem Israel; and besides all this, it is now the third day since this took place. Some women from our group, however, have astounded us: they were at the tomb early in the morning and did not find his body; they came back and reported that they had indeed seen a vision of angels who announced that he was alive. Then some of those with us went to the tomb and found things just as the women had described, but him they did not see." And he said to them, "Oh, how foolish you are! How slow of heart to believe all that the prophets spoke! Was it not necessary that the Messiah should suffer these things and enter into his glory?" Then beginning with Moses and all the prophets, he interpreted to them what referred to him in all the scriptures. As they approached the village to which they were going, he gave the impression that he was going on farther. But they urged him, "Stay with us, for it is nearly evening and the day is almost over." So he went in to stay with them. And it happened that, while he was with them at table, he took bread, said the blessing, broke it, and gave it to them. With that their eyes were opened and they recognized him, but he vanished from their sight. Then they said to each other, "Were not our hearts burning [within us] while he spoke to us on the way and opened the scriptures to us?" So they set out at once and returned to Jerusalem where they found gathered together the eleven and those with them who were saying, "The Lord has truly been raised and has appeared to Simon!" Then the two recounted what had taken place on the way and how he was made known to them in the breaking of the bread (Luke 24:13-35).

Every spring we enter a season of hospitality—bridal showers, weddings, wedding anniversaries, first Communions, graduations, confirmations, and ordinations. For many people, hospitality means planning parties, dinners, and receptions. Many of us like to serve as hosts for such events; maybe even more of us like to be guests. Both can be enjoyable and exciting.

We have often been told that we should be good hosts for Jesus Christ; that is, we should let Christ come into our hearts, into our lives, so that he can dwell there. Often we work hard to welcome Christ as our guest. This is never more true than when we prepare to receive our Lord in Holy Communion. As an older hymn puts it: "Soul of my Savior, sanctify my breast; / Body of Christ, be thou my saving guest."

It's not bad for us to prepare a fitting place for Christ in our lives, to act as host for him and welcome him whenever he comes to us. And yet, Christ is not content to be only a guest. He also loves to serve as host. Christ loves to give a feast for us to enjoy.

Christ became a host for those disillusioned travelers on the way to Emmaus. They had thought that Jesus would be the answer to all their personal and, above all, their national problems. He would be their liberator from Roman oppression, their victorious and glorious political leader. So they thought. Then his enemies killed him. The great "cause" that they had been following in Jesus lost its greatness, and they were crushed. Suddenly it was all over, and there was nothing left for them to do but set out for home, to return to their former way of life before Jesus entered their lives.

As they hiked along, they welcomed a stranger who explained what was wrong with their understanding of Jesus: "Don't you see?" he said. "Don't you see that it had to be like this? Was it not written? Isn't this what all the Scriptures are about? Don't you understand that the Christ had to suffer and so enter his glory?" And then, in the world's first religious education class, the stranger showed them how and why this was so, explaining the Scriptures from Moses to the prophets and everyone in between.

The hours and miles flew by. "We're home!" Cleopas shouted as the two disciples neared their destination. But their talkative companion suddenly bade them farewell and was about to continue on. "Stay with us," they insisted. (It was getting dark, and it wasn't safe to travel alone at night.) And their fellow traveler, who had powerfully entered their lives through his words, entered their home.

Later, at the family table—I say "family" table, because might not the unnamed companion of Cleopas have been his wife?—the disciples asked their guest to speak the blessing over the evening meal. Remembering it later, they realized that it wasn't so much the words he spoke—after all, they were the same words that every Jew said before meals—but rather *how* he said them. It wasn't so much the breaking of the bread, for every Jew broke the loaf in much the same way; rather, it was *how* he did it. And as the stranger prayed those familiar words and performed that common gesture, he didn't seem a stranger any longer. To the two disciples, it seemed like the miraculous feeding in Galilee, when Jesus took bread, gave thanks for it, broke it, and gave it to the hungry crowd. Yes, just like that . . . . But . . . could it be? And then he was gone, the one they had recognized in the breaking of the bread. Christ, their guest, had become their host. The two disciples began as hosts, but they were transformed into guests of the risen Lord. And because they had been his guests both on the road and at table, they were empowered to become hosts for the apostles in Jerusalem. After racing back to the city, the Emmaus disciples spread a feast of good news for their companions: they recounted what had happened on the road and how they had come to know the Lord in the breaking of bread.

This story is one of the brightest gems in the Gospel. It fairly sparkles with the light of the risen Christ. And in that light we glimpse not only Christ but also the ministry of early Christian missionaries. Saint Luke's entire account of Jesus and the travelers to Emmaus looks like what must have happened over and over again in the first century, as Christian missionaries spread out to preach the Gospel and celebrate the Eucharist.

According to Scripture scholar Herman Hendrickx, the experience which has colored Luke's account is "the reception of the strange travelling missionary. The group which welcomes him . . . hears from his mouth the message of the fulfillment of the scriptures in the death and resurrection of the Lord. They offer him hospitality. Together they enter into communion with the risen Christ in the breaking of the bread. So, Jesus who joins the two travelling disciples is the One who, concretely and visibly, adopts the face of [those] down to the present time in the performance of their ministry."[26] In a sense, Jesus in the Emmaus story speaks and acts as Christian missionaries and pastors have done throughout the centuries: he explains the Scriptures and shares the Eucharist with believers.

In this Gospel story we find early Christian preaching about Jesus placed immediately before the breaking of bread. "In its present form, the story reflects the pattern of early Christian worship. The self-manifestation of the risen One takes place through the two events of the exposition of the Scriptures and the breaking of the bread. These two events take place in every liturgy; word and sacrament are integral parts of a single coming of Christ to his own."[27] By insisting that the Emmaus disciples recognized Jesus in the breaking of the bread, Saint Luke probably was instructing the Christian community that they too could find the risen Lord in their eucharistic breaking of bread. And as at Emmaus, so now in every Eucharist: both Word and sacrament are integral parts of Christ's coming to us in our worship.

Thus, if we have ears to hear and eyes to see, every Eucharist is Emmaus. Every place where we celebrate the Eucharist is the holy house of table fellowship with the risen Lord. Every eucharistic celebration is our opportunity to recognize his presence in our midst, in his Word and sacrament. For there, we join the Emmaus disciples to look beyond the bread we eat, and see our Savior and our Lord; we look beyond the cup we drink, and see his love poured out as blood.

Today Christ sets before us the riches of his Word and of his table, just as he has set them before believers in every time and place. What he shared with the disciples at Emmaus, he shares with us here and now: he gives us himself in his teaching and in the breaking of bread. These are the gifts we receive in every Eucharist: Christ's teaching for our daily living and his Body and Blood for our strengthening.

During his earthly life, Jesus loved to serve as generous host of God's blessings for body and spirit; the Gospel stories of his miraculous feedings and healings attest to this. In his risen life, he continues to be such

---

[26] Herman Hendrickx, *The Resurrection Narratives of the Synoptic Gospels,* rev. ed. (London: Geoffrey Chapman, 1984) 85.

[27] Reginald H. Fuller, *Preaching the Lectionary* (Collegeville: Liturgical Press, 1984) 78.

a host, one who sets before us what we need to live as God's people. As we learn how to be gracious guests of Jesus Christ at his table, we learn how to live as his grace-filled sisters and brothers. But we also receive his invitation to become gracious hosts of God's blessings for others.

For the two disciples at Emmaus, their recognition of Jesus in the breaking of bread led to mission—they set out to tell others of their experience. When the reality of the Lord's resurrection finally dawned on them, they might have tried to capture the moment and save it, to savor it all by themselves. But they didn't. They immediately hit the road again, eager to share the good news with the fearful apostles in Jerusalem. Can we doubt that on their way there, their sharing of memories of Jesus made their hearts burn within them once again? In this way, God's hospitality to them at the hands of the risen Lord became their hospitality to others.

So it is with those who minister God's hospitality in Word and sacrament at the Eucharist. Because they have known God's lavish hospitality there, they accept a mission to extend that hospitality to the liturgical assembly, with hearts and hands and voices. As the late Fr. Godfrey Diekmann, O.S.B., my confrere at Saint John's Abbey, wrote in 1962, when the Second Vatican Council was just beginning: "The Eucharist is not static. The gift becomes the obligation. The Eucharist is something dynamic, a life that demands to be lived. We receive Christ for a purpose, not to keep him for ourselves but to give him to others so that they may recognize him in us."[28] Could it really be true? As you give Christ to others, they will recognize him in you? Yes, wonderfully true! The more you share the riches of Christ that you receive in him, the more others will see *him* in *you*! And this is never more true than in the liturgy, for "as in the days of the first disciples, so today Christ is most vividly and perfectly recognized in the breaking of the bread."[29]

It is the privilege of liturgical ministers to reveal Christ to their sisters and brothers. He chooses to speak and act through them in the liturgy. When they proclaim the Scriptures or preach the Word, they take Christ's place on the Emmaus road, recounting the wonderful

[28] Godfrey Diekmann, O.S.B., "The Theology of Worship," *Theology Digest* (Summer 1962) 140–41, quoted in *How Firm a Foundation: Voices of the Early Liturgical Movement,* compiled and introduced by Kathleen Hughes (Chicago: Liturgy Training Publications, 1990) 94.

[29] John D. Wright, "*Sperabamus:* A Meditation on Emmaus," North American Liturgical Week, 1961, 2–3, quoted in Hughes, *How Firm a Foundation,* 269.

deeds that God has accomplished in him for our salvation. When they lead the congregation in sung prayer, they take Christ's place, echoing on earth his Easter song of triumph to his Father in heaven. When they minister the holy gifts of bread and wine, they take Christ's place, setting before their fellow believers his Body broken for us, his Blood poured out for us. When they welcome their sisters and brothers to the assembly, they take Christ's place, enfleshing his invitation to come to the feast. When they prepare the liturgical environment, they take Christ's place, displaying a tiny bit of the glory of the risen Christ, the one through whom all things were made. When they speak the words and perform the actions of their ministry, they take Christ's place, enkindling in fellow worshipers the fire of divine love that warmed the disciples' hearts on the Emmaus road.

In all these ways and more, the liturgy makes the risen Christ seen and heard and felt in a world that needs to see his saving power, hear his life-giving Word, and be touched by his gentle compassion. "Whoever listens to you listens to me," Jesus told his disciples (Luke 10:16). During my deacon internship, an elementary school lad asked me: "Mike, are you Christ?" What a question! Well, no, of course not. . . . But were we not made images of Christ through our baptism? And doesn't our baptism commit us to live in such a way that people will see Christ to be alive in us and us to be alive in Christ? As composer Tom Conry's "Anthem" reminds us: "We are called, we are chosen, we are Christ for one another."[30] Jesus Christ has no hands or feet in this world but ours, no eyes or mouth but ours. If we do not make him seen and heard and felt in our liturgical assembly, he won't be seen or heard or felt there. And then how lifeless our worship will be.

But the only reason we can reveal the risen, living Christ in our worship is that we ourselves have first listened to him on our personal Emmaus road and shared abundantly in his sacred meal of Word and sacrament. The faith that empowers all liturgical ministry begins with our baptism, but it must be nourished throughout our life by meeting the risen Lord many times. And don't you often meet him in the words of faith and the acts of faith of other believers? We all cherish the words and deeds of faith-filled family members and friends that have become part of our own faith. Haven't you likewise been formed as a Christian

---

[30] "Anthem" by Tom Conry, refrain, in *Gather* (Chicago: GIA Publications, 1988) no. 298.

by the liturgy's songs and stories and sacraments? They were treasured and handed on by early Christian missionaries, whose experience seems to underlie Saint Luke's Emmaus story in the Gospel; their successors have handed on to every generation the words and gestures of Christian worship that they received from others. Even Jesus himself received the tradition of table prayer from his Jewish ancestors. But he had made this traditional prayer so completely his own that how he spoke the words and performed the gesture revealed him to the two disciples.

In a similar way, we have received the words and gestures of our service from past generations. But have we made them our own in such a way that they reveal us to be servants of Christ? Do we speak our words and perform our actions in such a way that they reveal us to *be* Christ for our fellow worshipers? Presiders are sometimes encouraged to be like clear glass vessels that do not obscure, but rather reveal, the content of the liturgy. And that content is the risen Christ. A fine crystal goblet enhances the appearance of the wine inside it, but the cartoon characters on a glass call attention to themselves. Everything you say or do in the liturgy highlights Christ's presence and work—or obscures it. In accepting the 1990 "People's Choice" award for best movie of the year, *Batman,* actor Michael Keaton noted that he had taken seriously some advice given him: "Let the wardrobe act." That's good advice for us, too, if by "wardrobe" we mean "Christ." For it was Christ that we put on when we were baptized, and baptism is the basis of all ministry in the Church.

Here we are in the realm of art. Liturgical ministers are *artists.* Fr. Virgil Michel, O.S.B., another Saint John's monk and a pioneer of the liturgical movement in this country, liked to say that all liturgical art must work toward the divine transformation of human beings into what he called "other Christs." He also believed that the liturgy itself is a living art that accomplishes this transformation. Thus he could declare:

> Both the priest and the faithful who participate actively in the liturgical mystery . . . become supreme living artists in proportion to the perfection with which their external words, gestures and postures reveal and enact the inner divine reality that is the essential nature of the liturgical worship.
>
> It is because the liturgy in action is thus living art of the highest possible kind, that no element of it is negligible, not even the slightest word, or gesture.[31]

[31] Virgil Michel, O.S.B., "The Liturgy and Catholic Life," TMs [photocopy] 221.

Now being an artist within the liturgy doesn't mean exhibiting perfection every time. But sometimes we are tempted to think that how we speak our very familiar words and how we perform our very familiar actions in the liturgy doesn't matter very much. But if we are God's artists who are to become more like Christ through our ministry, then everything matters a lot—for example, the priest's greeting at Mass, "May the grace of our Lord Jesus Christ, the love of God, etc." As I speak these familiar words while extending my hands in an embracing way, I like to think of myself as a herald for God, someone who has a wonderful message for the assembled worshipers. They've heard it a thousand times before, but they need to hear it here and now, from me. And the same is true for all words and actions of liturgical ministry—in some way they all herald Christ's Gospel and welcome people to his sacraments. Ministering at the Eucharist—every word and act of ministering—should help worshipers to recognize the Christ who is present in sacred words and actions. This presumes, though, that you have already found him there yourself, and continue to find him there.

Robert Hovda rightly observes that "the power of worship is that it be worship—common worship. And that means a God-consciousness so awesome, so strong, so powerful, that all participants are focused not on ourselves and our many splendid gifts but on our common and mysterious Source, on the only One who is Holy."[32] The one who taught the Emmaus disciples on the road and broke bread with them at table had that kind of God-consciousness as he did so. Must we not have it too?

Yet recognizing and revealing Christ is a process that lasts throughout a lifetime. This is why we must return again and again to our personal Emmaus road. There, in prayerful listening, we can receive the Lord's word of encouragement and strength. You need to be a frequent guest at the banquet table of his Word and sacrament in your heart, reflecting often on what you do in the liturgy, and why you do it, and how you do it. And as you recognize Christ's presence in liturgical words and actions, you will more clearly see his presence somewhere else, too. You will more and more recognize Christ's presence in those you serve, for they reveal him to you as well. They are the Body of Christ, worshiping through, with, and in him.

---

[32] Robert W. Hovda, "The Amen Corner," *Worship* 64 (March 1990) 173.

But often in our assemblies, and in each of us, there are areas which have been touched, but only touched, not *grasped,* by the mystery: "We have seen the Lord!" The Emmaus disciples clearly were grasped by the mystery of the Lord's dying and rising, and they were never the same again. If you have not been grasped by this mystery, can you really help others to be grasped by it? Yet sometimes you can be grasped, really grasped, by the Lord's paschal mystery. Haven't you experienced moments when a word or phrase in the Scripture readings, or in the prayers, or in the songs, or a liturgical gesture, or even the expression on someone's face, revealed Christ to you in a most powerful way?

One Palm Sunday, as I was ministering the Body of Christ, the choir was singing the third verse of the song, "We Remember" by Marty Haugen: "Christ, the Father's great 'Amen' to all the hopes and dreams of ev'ry heart. Peace beyond all telling, and freedom from all fear."[33] Yes, I thought: Christ present here, the great "Amen" to God's will for this world, even to death, still with us here, greeted by the "Amen" of the members of his Body in this world. . . . Tears came to my eyes.

We need God-given experiences like that from time to time, so that we may be grasped by the mystery of Christ's dying and rising, which is the mystery of *our* dying and rising. Such experiences deliver us from the demons of routine and boredom that beset and besiege. May you have many of these life-giving experiences of the risen Christ, for they are the foretaste of the paschal feast of heaven. Don't these experiences answer our questions,

> Who is this who spreads the vict'ry feast?
> Who is this who makes our warring cease?
> Jesus, risen Savior, Prince of Peace.
> In Christ there is a table set for all.

And isn't praise our heartfelt response?

> Worship in the presence of the Lord,
> With joyful songs and hearts in one accord.
> And let our Host at table be adored.
> In Christ there is a table set for all.[34]

[33] "We Remember" by Marty Haugen, v. 3, in *RitualSong* (Chicago: GIA Publications, 1996) no. 724.

[34] "In Christ There Is a Table Set for All" by Robert J. Stamps, vv. 3 and 5, in *Ritual-Song* (Chicago: GIA Publications, 1996) no. 916.

At God's eternal banquet we will take our places with the travelers to Emmaus, who felt their hearts kindled by the fire of Christ's Word; with Peter and the apostles, who ate and drank with the risen Lord; with God's servants from every time and place, who are called to the supper of the Lamb. All of us shall be welcomed as honored guests. How completely we shall be filled with God's love in Christ Jesus! How joyfully we shall know that we were part of something *grand* on earth—revealing Christ to each other by sharing the riches of his Word and sacrament together. Why not live *here* as if you believe it *now*?

10

Prayers for the Journey

In the pre-Vatican II days, the Church saw in each of the priest's Mass vestments a symbol and reminder of some Christian duty. That is why the priest said a set of prayers while he vested for Mass. These vesting prayers fulfilled an understandable human need to prepare oneself for important tasks by asking God's help. These prayers aimed to put the priest in a proper frame of mind and soul for what he was about to do.

Take, for example, the prayer for putting on the stole: "Restore to me, O Lord, the garment of immortality which I lost through the sin of my first parents and, although unworthy to approach Thy sacred mysteries, yet may I be worthy of everlasting joy." The stole, worn around the neck, was seen to suggest a yoke, the yoke of Jesus Christ, which is sweet and light. Such is the yoke which all liturgical ministers receive from Christ, to whom our ministry joins us in the liturgy.

Most of the cards and plaques with these vesting prayers have been relegated to bottom drawers of vesting counters or to church storerooms. But prayerful reflection by the priest celebrant and other ministers before the celebration begins is never out of date or out of place.

Here are some inscriptions for sacristy walls (or refrigerator doors or bathroom mirrors) that can help put you in a proper frame of mind for your important service to God and God's people.

Meditations

Whatever you do, in word or in deed, do everything in the name of the Lord Jesus, giving thanks to God the Father through him.

—Colossians 3:17

Servers, readers, commentators, and members of the choir also exercise a genuine liturgical function. They ought to discharge their office therefore with the sincere devotion and decorum demanded by so exalted a ministry and rightly expected of them by God's people.

—Constitution on the Sacred Liturgy, no. 29, in *Documents on the Liturgy 1963–1979: Conciliar, Papal and Curial Texts* (Collegeville: Liturgical Press, 1982) 10

Next to the Blessed Sacrament itself, your neighbor is the holiest object presented to your senses. —C. S. Lewis

This is the hour of banquet and song;
This is the heavenly table spread for me;
Here let me feast, and feasting, still prolong
The brief, bright hour of fellowship with Thee.

—Horatius Bonar, in *The Hymnal 1982*, no. 316
(New York: The Church Pension Fund, 1985)

We pray from the same base as we live. Our prayer reflects the way in which we respond to life itself, and so our prayer can only be as good as the way we live. —Esther de Waal, *Seeking God: The Way of St. Benedict*
(Collegeville: Liturgical Press, 1984) 153

Do what you can and then pray that God will give you the power to do what you cannot. —Saint Augustine

Good celebrations foster and nourish faith. Poor celebrations may weaken and destroy it. —*Music in Catholic Worship*, no. 6

Haste is the death of devotion. —Saint Francis de Sales

We are taught to perform in this world the symbols and signs of the blessings to come, and so, as people who enter into the enjoyment of the good things of heaven by means of the liturgy, we may possess in assured hope what we look for.

—Theodore of Mopsuestia, Baptismal Homily IV, no. 18, in Edward Yarnold, S.J., *The Awe-Inspiring Rites of Christian Initiation: Baptismal Homilies of the Fourth Century* (Slough, England: St. Paul Publications, 1971) 223

Good liturgical celebration, like a parable, takes us by the hair of our heads and puts us in a kingdom scene, where we are treated like we've never been treated before . . . because this is clearly God's domain, God's reign . . . where we are bowed to and incensed and sprinkled and kissed and touched and fed with a bread and cup that are equally shared among all.

—Robert Hovda, "It Begins with the Assembly," in *The Environment for Worship: A Reader*, Secretariat, Bishops' Committee on the Liturgy,

National Conference of Catholic Bishops, ed. (Washington, D.C.:
Publications Office, United States Catholic Conference, 1980) 38

What is this place where we are meeting?
Only a house, the earth its floor,
Walls and roof sheltering people,
Windows for light, an open door.
Yet it becomes a body that lives
When we are gathered here,
And know our God is near.
        —Huub Oosterhuis, *Zomaar een dak boven*
            wat hoofden, v. 1, David Smith, trans.
            © 1984 by TEAM Publications

Prayers

The Rebbe of Tsanz was asked by a Chasid: What does the Rabbi do before praying? I pray, was the reply, that I may be able to pray properly.
        —*Gates of Prayer: The New Union Prayerbook*
        (New York: Central Conference of American Rabbis, 1975) 3

Petitions for Ministers from Ancient and Modern Liturgies

Be consoler to all the ministers of the Church; to all of them grant
pity, mercy, and spiritual growth.
        —Petition in the Litanic Prayer for Clergy and People,
            The Euchology of Serapion of Thmuis

Let us pray for the universal episcopate, for the whole college of
priests, for all the deacons and ministers of Christ, for the entire
assembly of the Church. May God keep and protect them all.
        —Petition in the eucharistic liturgy's Litanic Prayer of the Deacon,
            The Apostolic Constitutions, VIII, 13

For all of us gathered in this holy place in faith, reverence, and
love of God, we pray to the Lord: Ry. Lord, hear our prayer.
        —From the Roman Sacramentary's "Sample Formulas for the
            General Intercessions, Ordinary Time I"

For this holy house, and for all who offer here their worship and
praise, let us pray to the Lord. Lord, have mercy.
        —From the Kyrie in the rite of Holy Communion, *Lutheran Book of Worship*

Father,
your son washed the feet of his disciples

as an example for us.
Accept our gifts of service;
by offering ourselves as a spiritual sacrifice
may we be filled with the spirit of humility and love.
We ask this through Christ our Lord.

> —Based on the Prayer over the Gifts from the Mass
> "For the Ministers of the Church"

Bless us, O God,
with a reverent sense of your presence,
that we may be at peace
and worship you with all our mind and spirit;
through Jesus Christ our Lord.

> —*Lutheran Book of Worship*

Father, all-powerful and ever-living God,
we do well always and everywhere to give you thanks.
You have no need of our praise,
yet our desire to thank you is itself your gift.
Our prayer of thanksgiving adds nothing to your greatness,
but makes us grow in your grace,
through Jesus Christ our Lord.

> —Preface for Weekdays IV

O send forth your light and your truth;
let these be my guide.
Let them bring me to your holy mountain,
to the place where you dwell.

And I will come to your altar, O God,
the God of my joy.
My redeemer, I will thank you on the harp,
O God, my God.

> —Psalm 43:3-4, reprinted by permission of
> HarperCollins Ltd. © 1993, Grail translation

O God, empower us for what is waiting to be done, guide us in the
doing of it, and uphold us until it is completed. And in it all may there
be honour and glory to you, through Jesus Christ our Lord. Amen.

> —In *A Book of Vestry Prayers,* compiled by C.N.R. Wallwork
> (London: Epworth Press, 1976) 76. Taken from *Worship Now,*
> David Cairns, ed. (Edinburgh: The Saint Andrew Press, 1972) 185

Lord our God, help us to give our minds to you in our worship, so that we may listen to what you have to say to us, and know your will. Help us give our hearts to you in our worship, so that we may really want to do what you require from us.

Help us give our strength to you in our worship, so that through us your will may be done.

In the name of Jesus Christ our Lord. Amen.

—In *A Book of Vestry Prayers,* compiled by C.N.R. Wallwork
(London: Epworth Press, 1976) 67. Taken from *Contemporary Prayers
for Church and School,* Caryl Micklem, ed. (S.C.M. Press Ltd., 1975)

Lord God,
be powerfully present in every word we speak,
every note we sing,
every action we perform,
so that in all we do,
you may be glorified,
through Jesus Christ, our Lord. Amen.

—Michael Kwatera, O.S.B.

Blessed are you, Lord God,
by your angels and saints in the throne room of heaven
and by your holy people gathered as the Church on earth.
I join with worshipers of all times and places
to praise your glory revealed in Christ Jesus
and to give thanks for your saving deeds.

Send your Holy Spirit, source of all our prayer,
to all who serve your people at the liturgy.
Help us worship you in spirit and in truth.
Guide the thoughts of our hearts,
the words of our mouths,
and the work of our hands,
so that our service may give you glory.

All honor and praise to you, loving Father,
through Jesus Christ, our Lord and brother,
in the power of the Holy Spirit,
both now and for ever. Amen.

—Michael Kwatera, O.S.B.